Nicholson's

LONDON

PUB

GUIDE

W9-BHV-238

ROBERT NICHOLSON PUBLICATIONS

A Nicholson Guide

First published 1981
2nd edition 1985
Reprinted 1985
3rd edition 1987
© **Robert Nicholson Publications 1987**

London Map
© Robert Nicholson Publications
based upon the Ordnance Survey
with the sanction of the Controller of
Her Majesty's Stationery Office, Crown Copyright reserved.

London Underground map by
kind permission of London Transport.

All other maps
© Robert Nicholson Publications

Compiled by **Judy Allen**

Illustrations by Barbara Huxley

Additional illustrations
by Basil Constantatos
on p4, 35, 93, 99

Robert Nicholson Publications
16 Golden Square
London W1R 4BN

Great care has been taken throughout
this book to be accurate, but the
publishers cannot accept responsibility
for any errors which appear or their consequences.

Typeset by The Word Factory
Rawtenstall, Rossendale, Lancs.
Printed and bound in Great Britain by
Scotprint Ltd, Musselburgh.

ISBN 0 948576 13 8

Contents

Pubs by area:

Pubs by special feature:

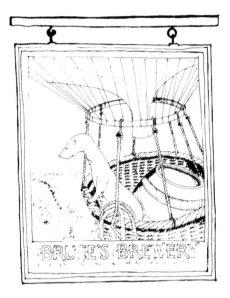

Unique sign showing London's longest pub name
'The Ferret & Firkin in the Balloon Up the Creek'

Introduction

Since the publication of the previous edition of this guide, the pattern of drinking in the capital has subtly changed. One of the agents of this change has been the relaxation of the licensing laws – traditionally as mysterious to foreign visitors as the game of cricket. Since the licensing laws first came into effect, drinking has been limited to two sessions a day, lunchtime and evening. The most usual London opening hours have been from *11.00–15.00* and again from *17.30 to 23.00*. There have always been the rare variations – for example, a few City pubs close as early as *20.00* due to lack of demand, even though they are licensed to remain open until *23.00*; and at the other extreme some entertainment pubs acquire special licenses to remain open until midnight or even later, and some market pubs have special licenses permitting them to serve alcohol to market workers early in the morning. However, since the new Bill, which came into effect on 2nd May 1987, pubs and other licensed establishments are allowed to dispense alcohol throughout the afternoon on condition that it is served to accompany a meal. A meal is defined as something which must be eaten with a knife and fork – a toasted sandwich or cheese roll will not do.

Those who run pubs must now decide whether to take advantage of this and to work longer hours to keep their customers happy. Those who decide in favour will clearly have to ensure that the food they offer is sufficiently substantial to qualify as a meal. This gives a tremendous boost to pub food, which had already been enjoying a welcome revival.

Alongside this change has come another, the rise of the brasserie, which tends to stay open all day and all evening, offering food, coffee and soft drinks during those hours when alcohol is off limits. The brasserie, and its older British counterpart the wine bar, is ideally placed to meet the new licensing requirements. This increased competition, coupled with the raised expectations of British people who regularly visit the Continent and enjoy its day-long open bars and cafes, is presenting pubs with a real challenge. Some breweries, notably Charringtons, have actually converted a few of their pubs into brasseries. Most are keeping the traditional pub character but turning it into something much more like the inns of old, which offered hearty sustenance of all kinds to travellers and locals.

The changes are not yet complete. A new Bill is presently under consideration which, if passed, will extend the licensing hours still further.

Sunday times, though, now and in the future, remain the same nationwide; *12.00–14.00* and *19.00–22.30*, except in strongly Methodist areas, such as parts of Wales, where pubs remain closed throughout the day.

Pub signs go back at least as far as the Romans, who marked each taverna with a vine bush, although you can't date a pub by its sign since many new ones built on older sites have kept the original name.

Ecclesiastical signs are among the oldest because many early wayside inns were hospices set up by abbeys and priories, and many early 'locals' were created to sustain the men building a new church.

After the Reformation the inns passed to the lords of the manor and were given heraldic names, like the ubiquitous Red Lion. Some of the more obviously Catholic names were changed – The Annunciation became The Hand and Flower, The Pope's Head became The King's Head, and from then on kings and queens were popular with sign-makers.

By the end of the 17th century, coffee houses, serving the newly imported infusion, were commonplace. Even then, many sold ale and by the 19th century most were pubs. In 1830 when ale was freed from duty thousands of ale shops opened and the gin shops competed by glamourising themselves into glittering gin palaces. 19th century property-developers built pubs as an investment – putting up the first to draw trade from workers constructing the surrounding houses. The last decade of the 19th century was when the big, classy Victorian pubs were erected. Today new pubs are still being built, on the site of former ale houses, or to serve a new community or leisure area. There are thousands of pubs – and numerous bars and brasseries – in London, and the following selection has been chosen to illustrate their immense variety. There are haunted riverside taverns with a grisly past, literary pubs, theatrical pubs, sporting pubs, pubs which go in for food in a big way, pubs with a real ale bias and, of course, entertainment pubs. Pubs have been associated with live entertainment since Shakespeare's time, when strolling players performed in the courtyards of inns, and 300 years later, music-hall was born in a pub setting.

To help you to choose, the guide has been divided into two main sections: areas of London, and pubs with special features. For the visitor, there is a brief introduction to each locality with details of transport facilities. Each pub listed has the name of its principal beer indicated as well as information on character, food, special brews, entertainment and facilities for children. There is similar information about wine bars, also arranged by locality, and a selection of reliable bars and brasseries.

This guide is designed for Londoners and tourists alike, to help them to get the maximum enjoyment out of drinking in the capital.

Symbols and Abbreviations

B – Bar food (from a snack to a full meal)
L – Restaurant lunch
D – Restaurant dinner
(Reserve) – Advisable to reserve a table
Closed **LD** *Sun* – Only restaurant closed
Jazz Sat – Evening for live music
Pub closed Sun – No drinking sessions on Sunday
Pub open to 21.30 – Time pub actually closes
(individual pub opening and closing times only shown
when they vary from the normal hours given below)
Priv rm – Private room for hire

Average cost of a pub restaurant meal for one inclusive
of VAT but without wine:
£ – inexpensive meal (under £7 per head for a three-
course meal without wine but including VAT and
service)
££ – £7–£15 for the above
£££ – £15 plus for the above

Normal pub hours Mon–Sat 11.00–15.00, 17.30–23.00.
Sun 12.00–14.00, 19.00–22.30.

THE BREWERIES

In the first edition of the London Pub Guide, we at-
tempted to credit each pub with the brewery it was tied
to. However, this proved confusing in the case of some of
the big national combines whose pubs are grouped under
trading names unfamiliar to most readers – whose only
concern, we believe, is 'what beer does it serve?' So, with
apologies to those combines who really prefer their full
and proper names to be used, we have simply answered
that obvious question. For example, if a pub is tied to
Watney Combe Reid Truman and is designated a
'London Host Group' pub, we have simply put
'*Watneys*', since that's whose beer you will be drinking.
Semi-Free Houses are also tied to Watney Combe Reid
Truman but serve other beers as well.

BLOOMSBURY & HOLBORN

W1, NW1, WC1, WC2. Bordered by Great Portland
Street, Euston Road, Gray's Inn Road, Oxford Street
and High Holborn. Bloomsbury is all about scholars
and writers, with its two great focal points – the
somewhat scattered buildings of the University of
London, and the huge columned edifice of the British
Museum, protecting the Elgin Marbles, the Egyptian
collection and countless other treasured antiquities.
The British Museum houses most of the books of the
British Library, until such time as its new premises in
Euston are ready, and it was here in the great domed
reading room that Karl Marx wrote 'Das Kapital'.
Holborn, too, has connections with learning. Gray's
Inn, one of the four great Inns of Court, is within its
boundaries, and another, Lincoln's Inn, lies just south
of High Holborn.

Tubes: Tottenham Court Road, Holborn Kingsway,
Chancery Lane, Kings Cross, Goodge Street, Russell
Square.

Bricklayers Arms   2 G 22
31 Gresse St W1. 01-636 5593. *Samuel Smith*. One of
only two 1983 CAMRA awards, given for the best pub
refurbishment in the country, was bestowed here in
recognition of the craftsman-made joinery, brick bars
and pleasing design. Two tap rooms below, elegant
lounge above, real ales and good bar lunches. **B.**

Cittie of York   3 I 23
22–3 High Holborn WC1. 01-242 7670. *Samuel Smith*.
Huge late 17th-century pub with one of the longest
bars in London. Broken up with cosy cubicles where
lawyers used to have confidential chats with their
clients. The large three-sided fireplace is still in use but
mystifies newcomers (the answer to the mystery is that
the flue runs under the floor). You can drink Old
Brewery Bitter drawn from a wooden cask and eat a
good bar lunch. Priv rm. **B.** *Pub closed Sun.*

The Dickens   **3 H 27**
16 Northington St WC1. 01-405 9705. *Watneys*. Pub
with a plain face but a warm heart. The single bar has
been rendered Dickensian with pictures of the writer
and his work on the walls. Usually full of legal eagles
and the men from the nearby Air Ministry. Reassuring
homemade 'comfort food' always on the go, with real
ale to accompany it. **B.**

Hercules Pillars   **3 I 24**
18 Great Queen St WC2. 01-242 2218. *Watneys*.
Civilised modern pub (rebuilt 20-odd years ago).
Particularly interesting buffet with real ales to wash it
all down with. Elegant surroundings – lots of mirrors
and brocade. Popular with businessmen and
freemasons. Food served at both sessions seven days a
week. **B.**

Lamb   **3 H 26**
94 Lamb's Conduit St WC1. 01-405 0713. *Youngs*.
Cheery Bloomsbury local, popular with some famous
film faces. Photographs of music-hall stars and
Hogarth prints decorate the wood-panelled walls. Still
has the original snobscreens. The antique music box on
the bar does work if you can lay your hands on an old
penny to feed to it. Home-cooked food. **B.**

Museum Tavern   **3 H 23**
49 Great Russell St WC1. 01-242 8987. *Free House*.
The local for the British Museum, the tavern attracts a
mixture of research students and sightseers. (Karl
Marx wrote here!) Pleasant Victorian interior, with
engraved glass windows and neat little tables at which
to eat your pub grub. Very crowded at lunchtime.
Afternoon cream teas served. **B.** *Open from
11.00–23.00 Mon–Sat, 12.00–22.30 Sun.*

Old Red Lion   **3 I 23**
72 High Holborn WC1. 01-405 1748. *Charrington*.
Rather proud of the fact that Oliver Cromwell's
headless body spent a short time within its walls.
Despite this gruesome note, it's a nice old bar with lots
of woodwork, engraved glass and windows. Upstairs is
the pleasant Cromwell Bar. Priv rm. **B.**

Peter's Bar   **3** G 25
Southampton Row WC1. 01-405 2006. *Free House*.
Very pub-like, although in fact it's part of the
Bloomsbury Park Hotel. Ground floor and cellar bars
both have Edwardian decor, lots of mahogany and
oak, and blackened beams. There are coal fires on the
ground floor in winter. Three real ales and Thomas
Hardy bottled beer, said to be the strongest you can
get. Basket meals all week and bar snacks Mon–Fri. **B.**

Plough   **3** H 24
27 Museum St W1. 01-636 7964. *Ind Coope*.
Edwardian and literary, as befits its Bloomsbury
situation. Long bar with wood panelling, dim lighting
and Tiffany shades. The haunt of publishers and
writers. On a corner site, so there is room for outdoor
tables and chairs along two sides. Restaurant upstairs
serves English food. **B L D**. *Closed D Sun*. **££.**

Princess Louise   **3** I 23
208 High Holborn WC1. 01-405 8816. *Vaux Free
House*. Large, welcoming Victorian pub on two floors,
all heavy dark mahogany, polished brass, tiles and
engraved glass, which won the London Evening
Standard Pub of the Year Award in 1986. Very good
on the real ale front, with Vaux's own Northern bitters
and good guest beers. Nice food at every session –
more choice at lunchtime than in the evening, because
that's when the demand arises. **B.**

Ship Tavern   **3** I 25
12 Gate St WC2. 01-405 1992. *Youngers*. The oldest
parts, including the cellar with its blocked-off priest's
hole, are 16th century, but other bits have been added
and changed over the years. Very decorative ceiling.
Full of legal types from nearby Lincoln's Inn Fields.
Separate restaurant does grills and steaks. Priv rm. **B L**
(Reserve). *Pub closed Sat & Sun*. **£.**

The Thunderer   **3** H 28
59 Mount Pleasant WC1. 01-837 6114. *Whitbreads*.
Just outside the area, on the other side of Gray's Inn
Road, and virtually next door to the Post Office HQ.
The theme is *The Times*, known as *The Thunderer* in

days of past glory; photographs and old editions cover the walls. Go upstairs for Flicks Wine Bar with its photos of old movie stars and full meals. **B L. £.**

White Horse **6** J 25
St Clement's Lane WC2. 01-242 5518. *Whitbread.* This is a darts and real ale pub (Fremlin's Tusker and Wethered's Bitter) which attracts businessmen, and tourists who have been examining The Old Curiosity Shop in the street behind. Newly decorated in olde worlde style with law pictures. **B.** *Closed Sat eve & all Sun.*

CAMDEN TOWN, KENTISH TOWN & NORTH WEST LONDON

NW1, NW2, NW5, NW6. Camden Town and Kentish Town form a line from Euston Road north to Archway. This section also includes pubs in areas roughly south and west of Hampstead, and north and west of Marylebone and Paddington, such as Kilburn and, further north, Cricklewood. It is a huge and very mixed area, partly run down, partly up-and-coming, mainly residential, with high streets catering for the shopping needs of a mixed race population. Different communities tend to congregate in specific areas – Kilburn, for instance, has a great many Irish, while Camden with its cheerful late night tavernas has many Greeks.

Tubes: Camden Town, Kentish Town, Kilburn, West Hampstead, Chalk Farm, Harlesden.

Assembly House
292–4 Kentish Town Rd NW5. 01-485 2031. *Truman.* An earlier inn on this site was an assembly point for travellers, who set out in convoy to outface highwaymen. Was once also an assembly point for a film crew who shot part of 'The Villains', with Richard

Burton, here. On a more elevated note – T. S. Eliot drank here. Pleasant Victorian interior with lovely mirrors and interesting woodwork. **B.**

The Belmont
78–79 Chalk Farm Rd NW1. 01-267 5017. *Watneys.* Small, pleasant and often full of music people and models from the nearby recording and photographic studios. Websters and Ruddles ales, as well as Watneys, several wines and lots of food – steaks cooked to order, sandwiches made while you watch. **B.**

Eliza Doolittle   3 C 26
3 Ossulton St NW1. 01-387 0836. *Ind Coope.* Named after the heroine of Bernard Shaw's 'Pygmalion', who is possibly better known for her role in the musical version 'My Fair Lady'. Inoffensive reproduction Victoriana, with glass shaded lights, booths and modern wood panelling. Very crowded at lunchtime with office workers in search of good snacks. One of the few places where you can eat Humble Pie and enjoy it. **B.**

Grand Junction Arms
Acton Lane NW10. 01-965 5670. *Youngs.* Big old pub on the Grand Junction Canal with two canal-side gardens where barges tend to draw up for refreshments. Often has barbecues in summer. Full meals at lunch-time and snacks in the evening. **B L. £.**

Prince of Wales
37 Fortune Green Rd NW6. 01-435 0653. *Watneys.* Upstairs, a spacious glass-roofed conservatory overlooks the sheltered garden, where barbecues are cooked in fine weather. The airy ground floor bar attracts a young crowd, mainly because of the Fri and Sun night discos and the live music on a Sat night. **B.**

Production Village
108 Cricklewood Lane NW2. 01-450 9361. *Charrington.* Production Village is a film studio and though they still make films here they've turned it into a setting for a perfect family outing – there's something for everyone. There are two pubs. The Magic Hour, a reconstructed Victorian pub with gas lamps and a log

fire, which serves traditional English fare both sessions seven days a week and features a pianist every evening. The Hog's Grunt, a reconstructed barn, has a late licence to *02.00* and offers jazz, rock'n'roll and funk seven nights a week. The Village restaurant is called the Odd-plate and offers fine food made from fresh ingredients and also an intimate cocktail bar. If that isn't enough there is also a 100-seat theatre for fringe productions and late-night cinema, again every night, licensed to *24.00*. For the children there is a full puppet theatre and a family room is planned. At the centre of the complex is the village pond complete with ducks and weekend barbecues and pig-roasts in summer. Function, conference and banqueting facilities for up to 500 people are also available. **B L D** *(Reserve Sat & Sun)*. **££.**

Sir Robert Peel
108 Malden Rd NW5. 01-485 2673. *Watneys*. Large and reliable one-bar house next to a busy street market. A snack bar for cold cuts at lunchtime, a reasonable selection of wines and a garden out at the back if you want to take the air. **B.**

THE CITY ═══════════

EC1, EC2, EC3, EC4. The 'square mile' of the City is the oldest part of London, the seed from which all the rest grew. It is built on two hills, Ludgate Hill and Cornhill, and the remains of the Roman wall which once surrounded it are still in evidence. With eyes lowered you see the medieval street plan, the tiny alleyways and old churchyards and taverns which survived the Great Fire of 1666. With eyes raised you see the glittering cliffs of modern buildings, which now dwarf the once massive dome of St Paul's. The major developments in London's old docklands are beginning to change the face of the waterfront to the east of the City and the 1987 opening of the new City Airport for short-haul flights will mean that a City

business-person is not much more than an hour away
from a European counterpart. In the very early
morning the area around the great meat market at
Smithfield is the centre of traditional buying and
selling. A little later – but only a little later – the ancient
streets and modern buildings are full of those engaged
in banking, insurance, stockbroking and other modern
forms of buying and selling. The City has become even
more high-tech since the Big Bang, but its archaic
pageantry still survives. Each November crowds
gather to watch the Lord Mayor's Show with its
procession of elaborate floats accompanied by the
Mayor (second only to the Sovereign within the City
boundaries) in a golden coach. All year round tourists
flock to the Tower with its gruesome history,
traditional Yeomen Warders and Ceremony of the
Keys, and its important charge – the Crown Jewels.
Busy and lively by day the City is still quiet in the
evenings and at weekends, apart from the traffic
around the Barbican Arts Centre, and many of its
drinking establishments close early and remain closed
over Sat and Sun.

Tubes: Blackfriars, Mansion House, Cannon Street,
Monument, Tower Hill, Aldgate, Liverpool Street,
Bank, St Paul's, Barbican, Moorgate.

Barley Mow   **6** K 29
50 Long Lane EC1. 01-606 6591. *Free House*. Built on
the site of a former monastery, this 400-year-old inn is
a free house specialising in real ales and bitters.
Popular meeting place for the meat market. Two bars,
stylish Edwardian interior and exposed beams. Home-
made bar snacks. Priv rm. **B.** *Pub closed Sat & Sun*

Bishop's Finger (The Rutland)   **6** K 29
9/10 West Smithfield EC1. 01-248 2341. *Shepherd
Neame*. Here we have good beer and an identity crisis.
The correct name is The Rutland but a plan to change it
to that of one of Shepherd Neame's beers resulted in
Bishop's Finger not only being painted on the front,
but also catching on. People from the City and the Old
Bailey mingle with the odd blood-stained meat porter

in the two bars, or spill out to drink at the edges of the park opposite. **B.** *Pub closed Sat & Sun.*

Blackfriar   **6 M 28**
174 Queen Victoria St EC4. 01-236 5650. *Free House.* Triangular shaped building in the shadows of Blackfriars railway bridge, with arguably one of the richest and strangest pub interiors in London. Saloon bar is like an art nouveau temple of marble and bronze, with beaten bronze bas-reliefs of friars singing and working. Off it, there is an even more stunning 'side chapel' for cosier drinking, with an arched mosaic ceiling, red marble columns, and more friars – this time accompanied by crouching demons, fairies and alabaster animals. The public bar is less ornate and this is where the food is; hot and cold at lunchtime, cold buffet in the evening. Beers include Adnam's, Bass and Tetley's. **B.** *Pub open to 22.00. Closed Sat & Sun.*

The Blackfriar

Bull's Head   6 O 32
80 Leadenhall St EC3. 01-283 2830. *Charrington*.
Small, popular pub, rebuilt in the 19th century on one
of the oldest pub sites in the City. Reputedly serves the
cheapest spirits in London. Said to be the Bull in 'The
Pickwick Papers'. Wine bar on the first floor has wide
selection, from table wine up to a good claret. Second
floor restaurant serves lunches – mainly French
cuisine. There is also an off-sales operation and, for a
reasonable fee, you can book in for a wine-tasting
evening. Priv rm. **B L** *(Reserve). Pub open to 21.30.
Closed Sat & Sun.* **££.**

Butler's Head   6 M 31
11 Telegraph St EC2. 01-606 2735. *Free House*. One of
the few remaining pubs to remember Dr William
Butler who, although unqualified, became physician at
the court of James I. His medicinal ale had the
reputation of being a cure-all and the inns which sold it
hung out signs bearing his picture by way of
advertisement. When demand for the ale declined,
most of the pubs changed their names. This one, which
didn't, has a large horseshoe bar, a doubles bar, lots of
lights and a hearty City trade. Beers include Tetley's,
Boddington's, Bass and John Bull. **B.** *Pub open to
20.00. Closed Sat & Sun.*

The Castle   6 J 29
34 Cowcross St EC1. 01-253 2892. *Charrington*. The
sign outside, with its castle in the background and three
balls in front, gives the clue that this is the only pub in
England with a pawnbroker's licence. Oil painting
over the bar shows the Royal Charter for pawnbrokery
being granted. Undoubtedly a useful facility for
anyone faced with an unexpectedly expensive round,
though apparently no one takes advantage of it these
days. Cheerful, basic pub with fruit machines and
jukebox. Priv rm. **B.** *Pub closed Sat & Sun.*

Cheshire Cheese   6 P 32
Crutched Friars EC3. 01-481 1533. *Charrington*.
Lurking under the railway arches of Fenchurch Street
Station, this pub conveys an appealing Victorian

atmosphere. Two floors, real ale, excellent bar snacks. *Pub closed Sat & Sun.* **B.**

The Cockpit   6 M 28
7 St Andrew's Hill EC4. 01-248 7315. *Courage.* Wedge-shaped pub, handy for 'The Observer' newspaper offices and Fleet Street. There was cock-fighting on the site in the past and the walls repeat the curious sight of two Courage emblems locked in mortal combat. Light food at both sessions. **B.** *Pub closed all Sun.*

Crutched Friars, Ye Old   6 P 32
15a Crosswall EC3. 01-480 5282. *Watneys.* Near the site of Crutched Friars Abbey and, interestingly, part of a Roman wall runs through the cellar. The friars may have taken their name from the cross of St Andrew, which was emblazoned on their habits or from the disabled brothers' recently disinterred from a nearby graveyard. Sadly, the pub is under threat of demolition. A friendly, busy pub, especially full at lunchtime. On fine days the overspill drink at tables out in Friar's Passage and admire the window boxes. Priv rm. **B.** *Pub closed Sat & Sun eves.*

Dirty Dick's   6 N 33
202 Bishopgate EC2. 01-283 5888. *Free House.* Has been cleaned up, and the mouse skeletons, mummified cat and other impedimenta which gave it its name have been relegated to a glass case in the lower bar. Still plenty of atmosphere in the all-wood galleried main bar and the slightly more informal downstairs bar. Gallery itself is a lunchtime wine bar, reached by an elegant spiral stairway. **B L** *(Reserve). Pub closed Sun eve.* **£.**

Hand and Shears
1 Middle St EC1. 01-600 0257. *Courage.* Sometimes called The Fist and Clippers. Either way, the name comes from the nearby Cloth Fair. At one time, magistrates used to hear cases in the room above. Nowadays it is a pleasant Victorian City boozer, and the 'local' for St Bartholomew's Hospital – which is why the pub scenes for the film of 'Doctor in the

House' were shot here. Priv rm. **B.** *Pub closed Sat & Sun.*

Hoop and Grapes   **6** P 33
47 Aldgate High St EC3. 01-480 5739. *Charrington.* A courteously restored 13th-century inn, believed to be the oldest non-ecclesiastical building in the City. The new wooden furniture and the conservatory corner are entirely in keeping with the venerable timber-framed structure. Hot lunches on weekdays. **B.** *Pub closed all Sat & Sun eve.*

Jamaica Wine House   **6** N 31
St Micheal's Alley, Cornhill EC3. 01-626 9496. *Free House.* The first coffee house to be opened in London. It was destroyed in the Great Fire, rebuilt by Wren in 1668, slightly damaged by another fire in 1748 and restored in 1858. The two bars are as different as if they belonged to separate pubs. Upstairs there is oak-panelling, lino, plain seats, wines, ports, spirits, lagers and businessmen. Downstairs there is carpeting, tables, comfortable chairs, draught beer and a 'public bar' atmosphere. **B.** *Pub open to 20.00. Closed Sat & Sun.*

Lamb Tavern   **6** O 31
Leadenhall Market EC3. 01-626 2454. *Youngs.* First built in 1780, rebuilt in 1881, and refurbished in 1986 without damage to the Victorian character, this pub stands right in Leadenhall Market. Very much a businessman's haunt with a devoted band of regulars. Its first floor bar is the first in the City to ban smoking. Mentioned in the Pickwick Papers and a little more recently used in the filming of 'Winds of War' with Robert Mitchum. **B.** *Pub open to 21.30. Closed Sun.*

The Lord Nelson   **6** J 32
264 Old St EC1. 01-253 3558. *Watneys.* A happy mix of old oak and pewter with TV, darts and pool. There's always food, cold or microwaved, with imaginative salads. Very friendly, with large benign dog. **B.**

Ludgate Cellars   **6** L 27
Apothecary St EC4. 01-236 6808. *Whitbread.* Large, rambling, congenial beer and wine bar which goes right

through to another entrance/exit in Blackfriar's Lane. Candles stand on beer barrels and wine bottles are stacked near the ceiling. Three large, linked bars, incorporating a restaurant and snack bar, take most of the space, with four small side rooms for cosy chats. Despite its subterranean situation, there is a sense of space and of freedom to wander. Four priv rms. **B L** *(Reserve). Pub open to 20.30 Mon–Wed, to 23.00 Thur–Fri. Closed Sat & Sun.* **££.**

Magogs   6 M 30

8 Russia Row EC2. 01-606 3293. *Free House.* Modern circular pub which was built to replace the old Gog and Magog, bombed in the war. Outside the front door are effigies of Gog and Magog, the giants who guard the City of London. Large but crowded ground floor bar. Downstairs is Micawber's wine bar. Drink Bass, Everards and Keg Bitters and enjoy home-cooked food at lunchtime and in the evening. Priv rm. **B.** *Pub closed Sat & Sun.*

Magpie and Stump   6 L 28

18 Old Bailey EC4. 01-248 3819. *Charrington.* Pleasant old pub, partially rebuilt in 1931. In the quieter back bar crime reporters and barristers gather after a session at the Old Bailey opposite. The front bar attracts the friends and family of the convicted or acquitted. Upstairs, a long bar called Court No 10 when the Old Bailey had 9, but not renamed Court 24 now the Old Bailey has 23! When old Newgate Prison still stood opposite, the gentry used to hire window space here to watch the public hangings. Upstairs is a restaurant serving traditional English food with a special 'hanging breakfast' on Sun morning. **B L D.** *Pub closed Sat.* **££.**

Old King Lud   6 L 28

78 Ludgate Hill EC4. 01-236 6610. *Whitbread.* Named after the legendary chief of the Ancient Britons, whose carved face gazes woodenly out over the main door. Long, low-ceiling'd, with hand-pumped beer, etched windows, original prints and loud taped music. The cellars once formed part of Newgate Prison and the building itself served as town house for the Lord Mayor

of London before it became a coaching inn at the turn of the 19th century. Part of the pub has been made into a Pizza Hut restaurant. **B L.** *Closed Sat & Sun eves.* **£.**

Penny Black   **6 L 31**
Tentor House, Moorfields, Moorgate EC2. 01-628 3675. *Free House.* Good stamping ground for philately enthusiasts. Decorated with top-quality photostats of an enormous number of stamps, all supplied by the GPO Museum which houses the originals. Reliable pub grub and traditional ales. **B.** *Pub open to 20.30. Closed Sat & Sun.*

The Pumphouse   **6 O 31**
86 Fenchurch St EC3. 01-481 1177. *Charrington.* Large new basement pub, handy for Lloyds. Cosy and crowded. Real ale and Mr Toby's pantry for food. **B.** *Pub closed Sat & Sun.*

Railway Tavern   **6 N 33**
15 Liverpool St EC2. 01-283 3598. *Whitbread.* Not only is it opposite Liverpool Street Station, it is also a railway 'theme' pub. Pictures of tube trains in the games room, a frieze of the coats of arms of the railway companies over the main bar, and model trains, prints, photographs and advertisements in the wine bar. Priv rm. **B.** *Pub open to 21.00. Closed Sat & Sun.*

Ship and Turtle   **6 O 32**
P & O Building, Leadenhall St EC3. 01-283 5485. *Courage.* Underneath the P & O Building this wine and ale bar dispenses traditional beers by the jugful, a selection of house wines, and spirits if called for. Looks like a wine bar, with its wooden floor, Victorian mahogany and bull's-eye glass, but most people come for the beer. **B.** *Pub open to 21.00. Closed Sat & Sun.*

Ship Tavern   **6 O 31**
27 Lime St EC3. 01-626 7600. *Truman.* A real old wood-panelled City pub, said to have been built in 1447. The name was especially apt in the 18th and 19th centuries when ship owners and master mariners made their way here from the nearby Thames. Past

associations are commemorated with a 10-foot ship in a glass case on one wall, an oil painting of a ship on another, and a bar shaped like the side of a rowing boat. Shove ha'penny and darts are still played here. **B.** *Pub closed Sat & Sun.*

Sir Christopher Wren   **6** L 28
17 Paternoster Sq EC4. 01-248 1708. *Watneys.* Interesting pub, built in the 60s when the new precinct was finished, but with genuine 17th-century fittings, including the huge fireplace in the small bar. Large dining room that offers solid English food – what you might call 'club grub'. priv rm. **B L** *(Reserve).* *Pub open to 22.00. Closed Sat & Sun.* **££.**

Sir Paul Pindar   **6** N 33
213 Bishopgate EC2. 01-247 8275. *Charrington.* Once the King's Arms – now named after a 17th-century merchant and philanthropist who became a close friend of James I. Downstairs, 1980s Victoriana. Upstairs Cyril's Bar for pool and snooker. A pool league of City firms is run here. Pub grub, draught beer and cheeriness at both levels. **B.** *Pub closed Sat & Sun.*

Smithfield Tavern   **6** J 28
105 Charterhouse St EC1. 01-253 5153. *Charrington.* Rebuilt on an old pub site in 1857 to serve nearby Smithfield Market. Still has an early morning market licence from *06.30–09.00* when only bona fide market workers are allowed alcohol – stray tourists must make do with coffee. Piano and pool table are especially popular during the morning session. Fills up with businessmen during lunchtime, and opens or not in the evening, as the whim takes it. Priv rm. **B.** *Pub closed Sat & Sun and some eves.*

Tiger Tavern   **6** Q 32
1 Tower Hill EC3. 01-626 5097. *Charrington.* New house on the site of an old one, opposite the Tower. Watchtower Bar is plushy and velvety and has benches outside on Podium Walk. The mummified cat, found in an old tunnel during the rebuilding, is supposed to have befriendéd Queen (then Princess) Elizabeth I when she was in the Tower. Beefeater Bar, garnished

with swords and a juke-box, attracts the young. Grills and dish of the day in the Toby Grill which is open to *20.00.* **B L D.** *Closed* **D** *Sun. Pub closed Sun eve in winter.* **££.**

Viaduct Tavern   6 L 29
126 Newgate St EC1. 01-606 8476. *Friary Meux.* Glamorous Victorian tavern built in 1869 and named for Holborn Viaduct, the world's first flyover. Opulent interior with three large oil paintings – one of them damaged when it was shot by a First World War soldier; a beaten metal ceiling supported by a cast iron column; an ornate pulpit-like manager's office and gold leaf round the mirrors behind the snack bar. In stark contrast, six Newgate prison cells still stand beneath. Priv rm. **B.**

Watling, Ye Olde   6 M 29
29 Watling St EC4. 01-248 6235. *Charrington.* Old, oak-beamed tavern on one of the oldest roads in London. Rebuilt by Wren after the Great Fire and used as office and digs by men working on St Paul's. Pleasant, basic bar with dark wood and red lino. Bistro upstairs goes in for rice and pasta dishes. **B L.** *Pub open to 21.00. Closed Sat & Sun.* **£.**

Williamson's Tavern   6 M 29
1–3 Grovelands Ct, Bow Lane EC4. 01-248 6280. *Free House.* Jovial tavern, reputedly the oldest in the City (built in 1666) and said to mark its exact centre. The home of the Lord Mayor of London until the 18th century. Approached by way of a leafy alley and small courtyard with a couple of tables in it. Serves four real ales, and Guinness and lager on draught. In the basement is Martha's Wine Bar with an extensive choice of food and 40-odd wines. Priv rms. **B.** *Pub open to 21.00. Closed Sat & Sun.*

Ye Olde Mitre Tavern   6 J 28
1 Ely P1 EC1. 01-405 4751. *Taylor Walker.* The tavern was first built in 1546, by the Bishops of Ely, to house their servants. Although it was rebuilt, in the 18th century, it still has its olde worlde charm – the bar broken up into small rooms with panelled walls and

Ye Olde Mitre Tavern

gentle lighting. The cherry tree preserved in the corner was once on the boundary between Sir Christopher Hatton's lovely gardens and the Bishop of Ely's land. It is said that Elizabeth I once danced around it. **B.** *Pub closed Sat & Sun.*

COVENT GARDEN ⸺

WC2. Bordered by Charing Cross Road, Strand and Kingsway. Since the departure to Nine Elms of the famous fruit and vegetable market, and the conversion of the splendid Market Hall to a complex of shops and wine bars, the area has become a flourishing centre for arts and crafts of all kinds. All new developments trail clouds of controversy and this one is no exception. The current discussions centre around plans for a new piazza around the famous home of opera and ballet, The Royal Opera House. But not everything here has changed. The narrow streets and alleys contain an appealing mix of old fashioned specialist shops and new gift emporia as well as traditional pubs, churches, art galleries, studios, workshops and theatrical costumiers. Remains lively until late at night with people arriving at the nearby theatres and the Opera House itself, and eating and drinking in the various cafes which stay open to enjoy their custom.

Tubes: Covent Garden, Leicester Square, Charing Cross.

Cross Keys   3 I 23
31 Endell St WC2. 01-836 5185. *Watneys.* Downstairs bar a little like a high-class junk shop, with ferns in chamberpots. Upstairs bar a 'fakes gallery' with Picasso and Matisse well-represented. Also some nice prints and drawings. Priv rm. **B.**

Kemble's Head   3 J 23
61 Long Acre WC2. 01-836 4845. *Watneys.* A Victorian, gas-lit, ex-coffee house, named for John Philip Kemble, the actor-manager who once ran the Theatre Royal in Drury Lane. Decorated with prints and pictures of old theatres and of the man himself. A suitable watering-hole before or after a visit to one of the nearby theatres. Upstairs restaurant serves traditional English food. **B L. ££.**

Lamb and Flag   6 J 23
33 Rose St WC2. 01-836 4108. *Courage.* A 300-year-old pub, originally known as 'The Bucket of Blood' because of the bare fist fights that used to be arranged in the room upstairs. Downstairs could be rough, too – Dryden got the once-over here for writing satirical verses about Louise, Charles II's mistress. Now a popular, mellow bar. Particularly good lunchtime snacks and a noted strong real ale. **B.**

Marquis of Anglesea   **6 J 24**
39 Bow St WC2. 01-240 3216. *Youngs*. A serious
drinker's pub with a chequered history. It was changed
from inn to coffee house in the 18th century, converted
back to a pub in the 19th century, extended in 1858,
demolished in 1941 and rebuilt in 1953. The
home-cooked food served in the upstairs
bar-cum-restaurant has recently become a feature of
the place. There is waiter service in the evenings and a
pianist on a Sun night. **B L D. £.**

Marquis of Granby   **5 J 22**
51/52 Chandos P1 WC2. 01-836 7657. *Taylor Walker*.
Pleasant pub round the back of Trafalgar Square and
handy for the Post Office and pigeon-watching! Very
busy at lunchtimes, but there's hot food in the eves too,
and four real ales. This is where the Bow Street
Runners caught up with Claude Duval, who was
eventually hanged at Tyburn for highway robbery. Priv
rm. **B.**

Nag's Head   **6 J 23**
10 James St WC2. 01-836 4678. *McMullens of
Hertford*. This famous and lively Edwardian pub, with
its strongly theatrical flavour, is the first Central
London venture of these old-established brewers.
There are two real ales, two Hertford-brewed lagers,
draft Guinness and the home-made lunches include a
traditional one on Sun. (No food eves.) **B.**

Opera Tavern   **6 J 24**
23 Catherine St WC2. 01-836 7321. *Taylor Walker*.
Opposite the Theatre Royal, Drury Lane. Popular
with actors from nearby theatres and specialising in
pre- and post-theatre food – shellfish, home-made
pies, salads. Victorian character and colouring,
especially in the first floor snug. When bottles rattle in
the cellar some say it is caused by the vibration of
passing traffic, others that it is the ghost of a man
murdered and buried in the cellar at the beginning of
the century! Priv rm. **B.** *Pub closed Sun.*

Punch and Judy   **6 J 23**
The Market, Covent Gdn WC2. *Courage*. Opened

towards the end of 1980 near the site of the first English showing of Punch and Judy. Flagstoned basement with wines, Director's and Best Bitter, and a food servery. First floor, with balcony overlooking the Piazza, serving lagers, bottled beers and a certain amount of food. Pub sign and pictures reflect the theme of the name. **B.**

Sun Tavern   3 J 23
66 Long Acre WC2. 01-836 4520. *Watneys*. Little Bacchus heads, draped in grapes, peer at you from the facade as you approach. Inside, the one main bar is furnished in comfortable pub Victoriana, with red plush and polished woodwork. Upstairs, anything from a full meal to a swift glass in the Bacchus Wine Bar. Home-cooked meals served at both sessions. Equally popular with local businessmen and tourists. **B.**

Two Brewers   3 I 23
40 Monmouth St WC2. 01-836 7395. *Raven Taverns*. Small, friendly, oak-panelled and lined with theatre programmes and playbills. Regular following of locals seasoned with theatre-goers and tourists, who enjoy quiet, gentle drinking. Many years ago, when it was called The Sheep's Head, a freshly severed sheep's head was hung outside daily. Happily, nobody chooses to impale two brewers on the doorposts. Priv rm. **B.**

White Hart   3 I 24
191 Drury Lane WC2. 01-242 3135. *Charrington*. Reputed to be the oldest pub in Covent Garden, possibly even the longest serving pub in London. Extensively restored with a cosy seating area in the rear for food and wine. They have recently reinstated their Tue evening middle-of-the-road jazz sessions. **B.**

White Swan   5 J 22
14 New Row WC2. 01-836 3291. *Charrington*. Housed in an attractive Queen Anne building. Front bar decorated with old mirrors and prints and called the Wine Bar, though the range is small and beers and spirits are also on sale. Back bar oak-panelled and hung with engravings. Priv rm. **B.** *Pub closed Sun.*

EARLS COURT & NOTTING HILL GATE

W2, W8, W11, SW5, SW6. For many people the name Earls Court is synonymous with exhibitions. The huge Exhibition Hall stands opposite the tube station, and only two blocks outside the area stands that other even larger exhibition hall – Olympia. Between them, they house Crufts Dog Show, The Royal Tournament, The Festival for Mind, Body and Spirit and other equally diverse spectacles. Earls Court itself is a mixed cosmopolitan area, with a high proportion of bedsitters and so many expatriate Australians that it has been nicknamed Kangaroo Valley. North across the elegant buildings and rich green of Holland Park is Notting Hill Gate – another cosmopolitan area, this time with a strong West Indian bias. Every August bank holiday the streets come vividly alive with steel bands, elaborate floats and dazzlingly beautiful costumes, as the Notting Hill Carnival bursts into action. A more regular source of street entertainment is the weekly Portobello Road antique market, where you are as likely to exchange a lot of money for something worth very little, as very little money for something worth a lot.

Tubes: West Brompton, Earls Court, Holland Park, Notting Hill Gate.

Blenheim Arms
Blenheim Cres W11. 01-727 8795. *Whitbread.* Friendly family house near the Portobello Road market. Specially busy at Sat lunchtime when stall owners and tourists gather to drink Flowers' Original and fortify themselves with bar snacks. **B.**

Colony
175 Westbourne Grove W11. 01-229 1774. *Whitbread.* A spacious and unusually pretty pub decorated with an abundance of trailing plants and with a white latticed glass frontage. Seating outside in summer. Lots of lunchtime food from Mon–Sat. **B.**

Duke of Norfolk
202 Westbourne Grove W11. 01-229 3551. *Watneys.*
Rather traditional, with a stag's head and old prints on
the walls and the food counter cut off from the rest by a
Welsh dresser. Quiet juke-box. Lots of tourists and
antique dealers. **B.**

Fulham Tap   1 F   2
North End Rd SW6. 01-385 3847. *Charrington.* At one
end of the lively North End Road market and recently
'done up' as a theme pub – the theme being brewing.
The food bar is busy morning and evening and there is
a special children's room and a nice garden so the
whole family can be made welcome. Draught Bass and
IPA, too. **B.**

Finch's (Duke of Wellington)   1 A   8
179 Portobello Rd W11. 01-727 6727. *Free House.*
Cheerful pub with trompe l'oeil windows painted on its
outside. In Portobello Road market so people
naturally gravitate outside to do their drinking in fine
weather. Not that it isn't very nice inside with its wood
panelled bar and occasional accordion player. **B.**

Sun in Splendour   1 A   8
7 Portobello Rd W11. 01-727 6345. *Charrington.*
Villagey pub, very lively on Saturday after the market.
Small courtyard easily gets overcrowded but people
spread all over the pavement regardless. Good food
and atmosphere. **B.**

Tournament   1 I   7
344 Old Brompton Rd SW5. 01-370 2449. *Whitbread.*
Modern pub right next door to Earls Court Exhibition
Centre, its name suggested by the annual Royal
Tournament. Mock-Tudor games room with pool,
darts and video machines, and a slightly plushy lounge
with military pictures decked around it. Good standard
pub food served at every session. and Wethered's
Bitter to imbibe. Priv rm. **B.**

Uxbridge Arms   1 B   7
13 Uxbridge St W8. 01-727 7326. *Whitbread.* In
harmony with this little enclave of small-scale peaceful

roads behind Notting Hill Gate – low-beamed, pretty and gently convivial. Good food weekday lunchtimes. **B.**

EAST LONDON ━━━━━━━━━

E1–E16. From the borders of the City eastwards, north of the river. East London is changing. Traditionally it has always been associated with slums, poverty, docks, warehouses, warm-hearted Cockneys, night-time violence and vibrant street markets. They are all still there but the horrifying bomb damage during the last war and the death of the docks have inspired major redevelopments which are fast changing the character of the area. St Katharine's Dock, at the west of the area, is now a marina with pubs, restaurants and smart private vessels; the old Royal Docks boast the New City Airport and extensive warehouse conversions and new development at Wapping and on The Isle of Dogs has created prestige offices and domestic apartments. But the famous Petticoat Lane Market is still lively, and many of the East End pubs go in for regular spontaneous sing-songs. It is true to say that all the pubs are friendly locals, but they are not all equally friendly to outsiders who come 'slumming it' from up West. Attitude is all-important, on both sides of the bar.

Tubes: Shadwell, Mile End, Bromley-By-Bow, Wanstead. Also British Rail from Liverpool Street and Fenchurch Street Stations.

Duke of Edinburgh
Nightingale Lane, Wanstead E11. 01-989 0014. *Ind Coope.* Tudor-fronted building next to Wanstead Hospital, which opens at *10.00* for morning coffee and serves three-course lunches in the saloon. Patio alongside, with its coloured fairy lights, means you can bring the children. Once, courts were held in the upstairs rooms of pubs – customers who know this landlord is a magistrate may be relieved to hear that

this no longer happens. There's usually a 'do' on a Sat eve and always free seafood at Sun lunchtime. **B.**

Five Bells and Bladebone
27 Three Colts St E14. 01-987 2329. *Ind Coope.* The 'five bells' used to be rung in the nearby docks to mark the time of *14.30.* The 'bladebone' may have been added because the pub was built on the site of an abbatoir and the bones turned up in the excavations, or because, when the abbatoir was operational, the bones were sold cheaply after the better cuts had travelled up West. Theme of the pub is boats, old tea clippers, and tools from the Port of London docks. **B.**

Prince of Wales
146 Lea Bridge Rd E5. 01-533 3463. *Youngs.* Large, lively and welcoming East End pub situated on the banks of the River Lea. There is a towpath for outside drinking in fine weather. Sometimes customers arrive with their own musical instruments, so if you take your harp to this party someone is more than likely to ask you to play. The Mikron Travelling Theatre performs here annually. **B.**

Royal Cricketers
211 Old Ford Rd E2. 01-980 3259. *Whitbread.* Large ground floor Victorian bar, smart and decorated with prints. A spiral stairway leads down to the canal-side bar with its fishing-theme decor and its patio . Popular with staff of the nearby London Chest Hospital. Children welcome. Hot and cold food at all times. **B.**

Spotted Dog
212 Upton Lane E7. 01-472 1794. *Watneys.* Handsome 17th-century inn used by city merchants during the Great Plague (when the name must have seemed somewhat tactless). Dick Turpin connections, though the decor keeps to a Tudor theme with oak beams, plaster whitewash and prints. Restaurant has a grill-type menu. Full of present-day city merchants at lunchtime but there is also a family room and garden. **B L D** *(Reserve Sat & Sun). Pub opens 19.00 Sat.* **££.**

Still and Star   6 P 33
1 Little Somerset St E1. 01-488 3761. *Charrington.* The

only one of its name in England, and set in 'blood alley'
where Jack the Ripper did his thing. Despite that, it's
cosy and comforting inside. Run by a Freeman of the
City of London who is not only a woman, but one of the
first women to hold a licence in the City. IPA on four
pumps – that's how popular it is. **B.** *Pub open to 21.00.
Closed Sun eve.*

Widow's Son
75 Devon's Rd E3. 01-538 0723. *Taylor Walker*.
Friendly one-bar pub in a slightly run-down area. Nice
Victorian glass, sea pictures and a piano that comes to
life at weekends. There was once a cottage on the site,
owned by a widow with a sailor son. As he was due
home one Easter, she made him a hot cross bun. He
never came, but each year she set by a fresh bun. The
pub continues the custom and each Easter a new bun is
added to the rather sad collection of ageing and
blackened confections. **B.**

The Widow's Son

The Windmill
20 Grosvenor Park Rd E17. 01-520 5198. *Whitbread.*
Pretty family local – a country-cum-City pub, despite
its location, with something for everyone. Strictly
there's only one bar but it's divided into little areas.
There are two snooker tables, a garden at the back and
at the side, a forecourt with seating, and some
up-market bar snacks (smoked salmon, crab and
prawns) as well as the usual lasagne and chilli. **B.**

GREENWICH & BLACKHEATH

SE10, SE3. Royal Greenwich once boasted a palace
which Henry VII enjoyed and in which Henry VIII was
born. It was magnificently rebuilt, principally by Sir
Christopher Wren, as a Royal Naval Hospital and is
now the Royal Naval College. But though it's lost its
palace, Greenwich is still rich in history and full of
interest and entertainment for the visitor. Here you
will find the National Maritime Museum, the world's
largest on its subject, housed in the Queen's House, a
Palladian masterpiece by Inigo Jones, and in two much
later wings joined to the house by elegant colonnades.
Here, too, is the Old Royal Observatory, on top of its
green hill, where you can see the Zero Meridian from
which Greenwich Meantime is calculated. The
Meridian Building and Flamsteed House, with their
exhibitions on navigation and time-keeping, are both
open to the public. The 'Cutty Sark', one of the
original tea clippers, and Sir Francis Chichester's boat
'Gipsy Moth' are both in dry dock here and may be
explored. Greenwich Theatre offers new plays and
classics, often with famous names in the cast, and also
has an art gallery above and a large restaurant, bar and
wine bar on the ground floor. There are classical
concerts in the beautiful Wren chapel of the Royal
Naval College from Oct to Apr and again during the
Greenwich Festival in Jun. This last includes concerts,

plays, readings, events and exhibitions involving most possible venues in the area, including the open air. Blackheath is an appealing village on the hill behind. For waterside pubs, check the **Riverside** section.

Access: Take British Rail from Waterloo station East, Charing Cross or London Bridge. By boat from Charing Cross Pier and Westminster Pier.

Coach and Horses
13 The Market SE10. 01-858 2882. *Ind Coope.* Lovely pub at the edge of a defunct vegetable market which has plans to turn itself into a mini-Covent Garden. Long L-shaped bar with coach-horse bits and pieces on the walls. Real ale and draught cider, generous salads, as well as nice hot meals. Occasional live music and discos. **B.**

Fox and Hounds
56 Royal Hill SE10. 01-692 6147. *Charrington.* Next door to the Richard I. It's smaller and more modest, attracting a generally older clientele – but extremely pleasant and amiable, with a beer garden, sandwiches available most times and hot snacks on weekdays. **B.**

The Gloucester Hotel
King William Walk SE10. 01-858 2666. *Charrington.* Next to one of the entrances to Greenwich Park (which means there are stunning views, but not from inside) is this spacious wood ceiling'd house, with interesting wood tables, pool, darts and hot lunches cooked on the premises (not Sun). **B.**

Hare and Billet
1a Eliot Cottages, Blackheath SE3. 01-852 2352. *Whitbread.* One hundred-year-old village pub, right on the Heath, with a pond in front. Very rural. Victorian wood panelling inside, hung with old prints of Blackheath and Greenwich. Was probably originally called The Harrow and Crooked Billet, if that's any help. Go through to the back for The Jugged Hare Wine Bar *(closed Sun).* Priv rm. **B.**

King's Arms

King William Walk SE10. 01-858 4544. *Courage.*
Large, smart and comfortable with gas-log fires and
really intriguing prints of sailing ships on the walls.
Eating area at the back overlooks the pleasant beer
garden. Fresh rolls and sandwiches anytime, hot
weekday lunches. **B.**

Princess of Wales

1a Montpelier Row SE3. 01-852 6881. *Charrington.* Sit
out at the front and admire the Heath, with a glass of
real ale at your elbow. Inside there's plenty of space
and good bar lunches. Popular boozer. **B.**

Ye Olde Rose and Crown

Railway Tavern

16 Blackheath Village SE3. 01-318 6637. *Ind. Coope.*
A good place to call in between exploring Blackheath
Village and striding across the Heath. Recently
attractively renovated and proud of being the fourth in
Britain for the sale of Burton Ale! The new light and
flower decked restaurant operates as a carvery seven
days a week and also serves three-course hot or cold
lunches from Mon to Sat. English food with some
Italian dishes – all prepared by an Italian cook. **B L D. £**
or **££.**

Richard I

52 Royal Hill SE10. 01-692 2996. *Youngs.* One of those
genuinely unspoilt places whose very traditionalism
has made it fashionable. No music, no carpets, no
one-armed bandits – just wall to wall regulars who
overflow into the back garden and out at the front on
fine days. Real ale, convivial atmosphere, and pub
grub Mon to Fri lunchtimes. (That's the only bit that's
not traditional – it's mostly burgers.) **B.**

Ye Olde Rose and Crown

Crooms Hill SE10. 01-858 0517. *Courage.* Friendly
pub with cheery bar staff, right next door to Greenwich
Theatre. Somehow has the atmosphere of a theatre
bar, with old playbills on the walls, gas-log fires and
fancy wrought ironwork. Meals anytime. **B.**

HAMPSTEAD & HIGHGATE

N6, NW3. Two hilltop villages on either side of
Hampstead Heath. High society came to the country
village of Hampstead in the 18th century when a
mineral spring was discovered and thought to have
healing properties. Most of the very attractive
buildings date from this period. Constable lived and
worked here, and so did Keats and Galsworthy.
Highgate began to grow at much the same time and was

home to Coleridge and A. E. Housman. Both retain their appealing village-like atmosphere and their literary and artistic connections – it is still fashionable for writers and artists of all persuasions to live here. Hampstead Heath (790 acres), which divides them, sprawls over sandy hills and dips into wooded valleys. Dick Turpin ranged over this Heath, and drank or hid in most of the local inns. To the north of the Heath stands the Georgian Kenwood House with its art collection and its grounds in which stands a lakeside, domed, concert platform. On summer evenings, eat a picnic on the grass while classical music floats across the water in competition with bird song and the occasional champagne cork.

Tubes: Hampstead, Highgate, Belsize Park, Swiss Cottage, Golders Green.

The Bull
North Hill, Highgate N6. 01-340 4412. *Taylor Walker.* 400-year-old inn that once supplied lodgings to Hogarth, Cruikshank, Landseer and Millais. The 18th century animal painter, George Morland, whose picture is in the bar, used to sit outside and contemplate passing coach horses. Popular with members of the English National Opera. There are chairs on the front patio, where Morland sat, and a paved tree-lined garden. Lunches *Mon–Sat.* **B.**

Duke's Head
16 Highgate High St N6. 01-340 6688. *Charrington.* 16th century coaching inn which still has the archway through which coaches passed to unload in the yard. Prints of the village hang on the old stippled walls, and the brass gleams a welcome. Made pretty outside with flowery window boxes. **B.**

Flask
77 Highgate West Hill N6. 01-340 3969. *Ind Coope.* Famous, olde worlde Highgate tavern named for the flasks which people used to buy here to fill with water at the Hampstead wells. Dick Turpin once hid in the cellars and William Hogarth drew in the bar. English restaurant offers both à la carte and set menus, always

including a roast of the day. Large forecourt for outside drinking. **B L** *Mon–Fri (Reserve)*. **£.**

Holly Bush
22 Holly Mount, off Heath St NW3. 01-435 2892. *Benskins*. Picturesque village pub dating back to 1796. Rumour has it that the overthrow of Cromwell was plotted within these walls. Genuine Victoriana in the main bar, pub Victoriana elsewhere. Burton Ale on draught. **B.**

Horse and Groom
68 Heath St NW3. 01-435 3140. *Youngs*. Quite an imposing exterior leads into an Edwardian interior with sepia pictures of Hampstead clustered on the walls. Anything from a snack to a casserole at the bar. Upstairs, Boris' Cocktail Bar, evenings only, where a glass of Boris's Bacchanalia will bring a falter to your step. **B.**

Jack Straw's Castle
Northend Way NW3. 01-435 8885. *Charrington*. Rebuilt in the 60s on the site of the original pub. Named for Wat Tyler's closest comrade who was hanged just outside. Unusual weatherboard frontage and marvellous views over the Heath. Courtyard with tables and chairs for sunny days. Snacks at the snack bar and inventive cocktails in the cocktail bar. Go upstairs to the Castle Carving Room for traditional roasts, game in season, and a trolleyload of sweets. Priv rm. **B L D** *(Reserve)*. *Closed* **L** *Sat*. **££.**

King of Bohemia
10 Hampstead High St NW3. 01-435 6513. *Whitbread*. Bow-fronted Georgian pub with a small garden at the back. Nice prints of old Hampstead around the walls. Fashionable meeting place for the locals. Good home-cooked snacks. Cheery and relaxing sort of place. **B.**

Old Bull and Bush
North End Rd NW3. 01-455 3685. *Taylor Walker*. Attractive 17th-century building, once the country home of the painter William Hogarth, who is said to have planted the bush in the garden. This is *the* Old Bull and Bush, made famous in the Florrie Forde song.

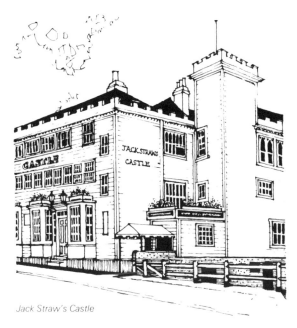

Jack Straw's Castle

There's a Florrie Forde Bar and lots of pictures of music hall stars around. Drinks on the pleasant forecourt in nice weather. **B.**

Rose and Crown
88 High St N6. 01-340 6712. *Whitbread*. 250-year-old pub reputed to have been used by Charles II – the small bar is still called The Royal Box in memory of his patronage. Honest boozer. Priv rm.

Sir Richard Steele
97 Haverstock Hill NW3. 01-722 1003. *Charrington*. Imposing Edwardian decor – faded plush wallpaper, oil lamps, and a stained-glass window of the essayist Sir Richard Steele. High percentage of regulars – quite a few of them actors. Bar snacks limited to sandwiches but you can drink IPA or Bass. **B.**

Spaniard's Inn

Spaniard's Rd NW3. 01-455 3276. *Charrington.*
Renowned 16th century inn, once the residence of the
Spanish Ambassador to the court of James I. The poets
Shelley, Keats and Byron drank here as did Charles
Dickens. This is where Dick Turpin stayed when he
was riding and robbing with Tom King. His pistols are
on display, as well as a musket ball he fired while
waylaying the Royal Mail coach. Delightful rose
garden for outdoor drinking. **B.**

Swiss Cottage

98 Finchley Rd NW3. 01-722 3487. *Samuel Smith's.*
Huge, popular pub, recently acquired and extensively
renovated by Samuel Smith's. The outside is still a
parody of a Swiss chalet – indeed, there is a
preservation order on its appearance because the area
and the tube station are both named after it. Inside
there are two large ground floor bars serving real ale
and bar snacks, a tap room and a large pool room with
six tables. Upstairs there is an à la carte restaurant
offering English food in the evenings, and an extensive
verandah bar. **B D** *(Reserve).* **££.**

Victoria

28 North Hill N6. 01-340 4609. *Whitbread.* Rather up-
market, turn of the century place with wood-panelling
effect wallpaper and brown button-backed seating.
Offers numerous delights including six real ales, a beer
garden at the back, a cold lunchtime buffet and hot
evening meals from Mon to Sat – and live jazz on Wed,
Fri and Sun nights. **B.**

ISLINGTON & HIGHBURY

N1. Both Highbury and Islington were fashionable
places to live in the late 18th and early 19th centuries,
and that is when many of their streets and terraces were
built. The areas began to decay a little in the early part

of this century, but more recently have become popular again and the attractive Georgian buildings are being restored and gentrified. Camden Passage near Islington Green, is well-known for its market and antique shops, and smart, expensive restaurants.

Tubes: Angel, Highbury and Islington.

Camden Head   3 E 32
2 Camden Walk N1. 01-359 0851. *Youngers.* Lovely Victorian etched glass in this busy, friendly one-bar pub on the verges of the Camden Passage Antique Market. Patio drinking in summer and reliable pub lunches from Mon to Sat. Traditional IPA is the best-seller. Priv rm. **B.**

Eagle   4 H 33
2 Shepherdess Walk N1. 01-253 4715. *Charrington.* Once a Victorian music-hall pub – in fact, the very one immortalised in 'Pop Goes the Weasel'. It still has an old world atmosphere, pictures of the music-hall stars, and a scale model of itself as it once was. Substantial snacks and basket meals at both sessions. **B.**

Giles   3 F 33
Prebend St N1. 01-359 6768. *Whitbread.* The moment you see the sign, with its awful Giles baby, you know that the pub is named after the 'Daily Express' cartoonist (who opened it in person). More Giles cartoons line the walls inside, most of them originals, and when you've read those you can play pool or darts or just have a friendly drink. **B.**

Island Queen   3 F 32
87 Noel Rd N1. 01-226 5507. *Charrington.* Three larger-than-life dolls dominate the bar in this very popular local. They used to wear lace-up underwear but are now more decorously dressed in Alice-in-Wonderland style. Four large leaded mirrors hang on the walls. No live entertainment as such, but something unusual often happens on special nights – like Hallowe'en, St Patrick's Day, etc. Get on the mailing list for details. Bar meals at every session, restaurant open for dinner from Thur to Sat. **B D. £** or **££.**

Lord Wolsey   3 E 30
55 White Lion St N1. 01-837 8505. *Samuel Smith*. Neat,
discreet and pretty. A home from home with open fire,
minute garden, real ale and wholesome bar lunches.
Wolsey, incidentally, was the General who reached
Khartoum two days after Gordon's death. **B.**

Ram and Teasel   3 E 33
39 Queen's Head St N1. 01-226 4830. *Whitbread*.
Victorian pub, convenient for the Camden Passage
antique shops. On Fri and Sat evenings there is a 50s
and 60s disco. **B.**

Rising Sun   3 B 33
55 Brooksby St N1. 01-607 2844. *Charringtons*.
Enthusiastically restored Victorian pub with small rear
garden. Original 18th-century prints of London line
the walls, there are genuine Britannia tables and the
IPA and Bass are pumped by real old brass and ebony
handles that date back to before World War 1. Bar
meals are on offer from Mon to Sat and light snacks are
available any time. **B.**

The Spurs
The Roundway N17. 01-808 4773. *Watneys*. Thirties
pub called after the football team Tottenham Hotspurs
– closer links are planned, including painting the pub in
the team colours. One old-world style bar with pool
tables, the other ultra-modern in which DJs from local
pirate radio stations host discos at weekends. **B.**

KENSINGTON, CHELSEA & FULHAM

SW3, SW6, SW10, W8. Bordered by the Thames,
Draycott Avenue, Cromwell Road and stopping short
of Earls Court Road. Kensington became important in
1689 when William III established Kensington Palace
by commissioning Sir Christopher Wren to rebuild an
existing house. It stands at one end of the lovely
Kensington Gardens which, together with the

adjoining Hyde Park, forms the largest open space in central London – 650 acres of it. South of the Gardens is a group of Victorian buildings honouring the arts and sciences, including the Royal Albert Hall. Kensington High Street is famous for its smart shops and department stores. Chelsea has a very different but equally famous shopping street in Kings Road, built as a private coach road for Charles II. This is where the adventurous search the boutiques for unusual clothes and the cautious sit in cafes and pubs to watch the results parade by. Parts of Chelsea have retained a village atmosphere and are haunted by the shades of writers and artists.

Fulham Road, parallel to the King's Road, also has its boutiques, restaurants and wine bars. Fulham Pottery, licensed in 1671, still stands, but the oldest building is Fulham Palace – once the residence of the Bishop of London, now ecclesiastical offices with its small but beautiful grounds and herb garden open to the public.

Tubes: Putney Bridge, Parsons Green, Fulham Broadway, Gloucester Road, High Street Kensington, South Kensington, Sloane Square.

Australian   **4** J 11
29 Milner St SW3. 01-589 3114. *Taylor Walker.* Victorian and basic – devoted regulars are prepared to commute to reach it and its real ales. Also has a good reputation for its food, available lunchtime and evening. Princes Cricket Club, which used to be next door, moved to Marylebone and became the MCC. So the name may have been inspired by the opposition. **B.**

Britannia   **1** E 6
1 Allen St W8. 01-937 1864. *Youngs.* Gentle, warm and friendly, with a pretty patio in which lives an ancient and well-established honeysuckle. Large bar with plenty of tables and chairs and, usually, fresh flowers. Proud of its beer, but also of its very good buffet. **B.**

Bunch of Grapes   **1** I 11
207 Brompton Rd SW3. 01-589 4944. *Free House.* Crowded and Victorian, with glass snobscreens separating the bars (so the coachman can't see how

much the lady of the house is drinking). Dark and woody with attractive painted mirrors. Four real ales, home-cooked lunches and evening bar snacks. Popular with locals, as well as tourists. **B.**

Chelsea Potter   **4** L   4
119 King's Rd SW3. 01-352 9479. *Watneys.* Used to be the Commercial Tavern until 1958 when it was renamed in honour of the Chelsea Pottery. The traditional mirrored interior has become a trendy meeting place for the Kings Road especially as it is open all day for snacks, coffees etc. Filling lunches are popular. Drinks go down well too. An 'alternative' juke box plays in the bar. **B.**

Churchill Arms   **1** D   8
119 Kensington Church St W8. 01-727 4242. *Fuller, Smith and Turner.* More snobscreens in this old-fashioned oak-wood interior. One side is given over to pictures of US Presidents, the other to pictures of English Prime Ministers, and especially Churchill. On-site chef to see to the grills. Glass conservatory at the back houses the landlord's collection of 1600 butterflies from all over the world. **B.**

Duke of Cumberland
235 New King's Rd SW6. 01-736 2777. *Youngs.* Elegant, Edwardian, and popular with the young and trendy. In the saloon bar – large mirrors, dried flowers

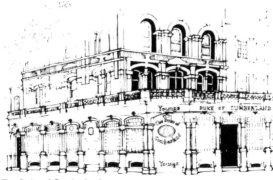

The Duke of Cumberland

and lovely Victorian tiles. Public bar designed to look like a stable, in sandblasted brick. Summertime drinking on Parson's Green opposite.**B.**

Enterprise   **4 J 11**
35 Walton St SW3. 01-584 8858. *Watneys*. Fashionable yet family pub, attracting some famous TV faces. Low-key pub games available over the bar – backgammon, chess, dominoes and cards. Real ale, and a separate food area with hot and cold meals. Benches outside. **B.**

Finch's (Kings Arms)   **4 L 4**
190 Fulham Rd SW10. 01-351 5043. *Free House*. Provides a good range of real ales. Fine, solid Victorian interior, with engraved glass partitions. Good pub grub at every session. Very arty crowd mingling happily with business types. **B.**

Goat in Boots   **4 L 4**
333 Fulham Rd SW10. 01-352 1384. *Watneys*. Dating back to 1887, this is a lively, young, French-managed establishment. Downstairs, at lunchtime a confident bistro-style restaurant which in the evening converts into a cocktail bar with an extensive list of concoctions. **L** *Mon–Sat*. **£.**

Greyhound   **1 E 7**
1 Kensington Sq W8. 01-937 7140. *Watneys*. Enjoy the friendly atmosphere in the front bar, or relax quietly at the back and watch the experts on the full-sized billiard table. Was destroyed in a gas explosion in 1977, but rebuilt in its own likeness in 1979. Plentiful food lunchtime and evening and seven real ales. **B.**

Hour Glass   **1 I 11**
281 Brompton Rd SW3. 01-589 9314. *Charrington*. Luxurious little bar, with velvet seating, white-wood panelling and two open fire-places where logs burn all winter. In summer there are tables and chairs on the pavement. Good range of food offered until *22.00*. **B.**

King's Head and Eight Bells   **4 M 8**
50 Cheyne Walk SW3. 01-352 1820. *Whitbread*. Has passed its 400th birthday! 18th century decor with pots,

jugs and prints of old Chelsea. Quite a few famous regulars. Permanent buffet with Wethered's or Flower's to wash it all down. **B.**

Peterborough Arms
65 New King's Rd SW6. 01-736 2837. *Charrington*. Huge, popular pile with wide windows which look across the road to Eel Brook Common. Light, glittery and very pretty. Bar food Mon to Fri, IPA and Bass on draught. **B.**

Queen's Elm   **4 K 4**
241 Fulham Rd SW3. 01-352 9157. *Courage*. So-called because Elizabeth I took shelter under a nearby elm in 1567. Refurbished olde-worlde interior with hot and cold food available at all times. Still popular with writers and publishers. Art exhibitions are held in the function room from time to time. **B.**

Surprise   **4 M 10**
6 Christchurch Ter SW3. 01-352 0455. *Charrington*. Might be called after the frigate that carried the body of Napoleon back to Europe or the ship that carried Charles II to safety – no one is quite sure. Prints and paintings of old Chelsea are all around the walls. Actors and football teams (rather than supporters) tend to stand around or lounge on the brown velvet seats. **B.**

KNIGHTSBRIDGE &
BELGRAVIA

SW1, SW3, SW7. A two-part area, bordered by Kensington Road and Knightsbridge to the north, Grosvenor Place and Buckingham Palace Road to the east, and to the south by a crooked line formed by Sloane Street, Pont Street, Beauchamp Place and the Cromwell Road. Knightsbridge was originally, like so many other built-up parts of London, a tiny village. Through it flowed the River Westbourne (now underground) and legend has it that two knights were once locked in mortal combat on the bridge over this river, and are remembered still in an area where today the only opportunity for mortal combat is likely to be at the Harrods sale. This is very much a luxury shopping area, although you may catch a glimpse of the military and their horses at Knightsbridge Barracks. In the days of the knights, Belgravia was rather different too – a fog-bound swamp patrolled by brigands. Today it is a stately residential area of squares and terraces, Regency mansions and foreign embassies.

Tubes: Victoria, Sloane Square, Hyde Park Corner, Knightsbridge.

Antelope   **5 L 13**
22 Eaton Ter SW1. 01-730 7781. *Benskins*. 18th-century inn that's become a bit of a rugby pub – hearty, companionable and beer-swilling. Wine bar on the first floor where you can get hot and cold food at lunchtime six days a week. **B.**

Duke of Wellington   **5 L 13**
63 Eaton Ter SW1. 01-730 3103. *Whitbread.* Traditional English pub on the borders of Chelsea and Belgravia. Dark green interior, with red lamps to give it a warm glow, military prints and a copper bar top. Pictures of the Iron Duke abound. Used by shoppers and workers as well as the Chelsea set. **B.**

Ennismore Arms   **1 H 11**
2 Ennismore Mews SW7. 01-584 0440. *Free House.* Small pretty pub in a cobbled mews. Neo-Georgian decor, an open fire, comfortable seating and good home-cooked meals. The roast lunches on Sun are going down a treat. **B.**

Grenadier   **2 I 14**
18 Wilton Row SW1. 01-235 3074. *Free House.* Once an Officers' Mess for the Duke of Wellington's soldiers. Full of military bric-à-brac, with a sentry box outside and the Duke's own mounting block in the passageway at the side. Tends to be haunted in September by an officer caught cheating at cards and accidentally flogged to death. Real ales and good English restaurant. **B L D** *(Reserve).* **££.**

Grove Tavern   **2 I 12**
43 Beauchamp Pl SW3. 01-589 5897. *Whitbread.*
Victorian gas-lit tavern with comfortable Chesterfield
sofas and military prints on the walls. Flower's,
Brakspear's and Wethered's Bitter to drink and hot or
cold lunches from Mon to Sat. Priv rm. **B.**

King George IV   **2 H 12**
44 Montpelier Sq SW7. 01-589 1016. *Whitbread.* Lively
pub, with dark brown and white exterior, hanging
baskets and outdoor tables. Stands in a street named
after a famous resort in the South of France because
this part of London was said to be especially healthy.
Don't be put off by the fierce warning sign against
trespassing – inside they are friendly and the snacks are
good. **B.**

Nag's Head   **2 I 14**
53 Kinnerton St SW1. 01-235 1135. *Ind Coope.* Looks
like a tiny corner shop from outside, small, cosy and

Star Tavern

cottagey inside. A bit of an actors' pub where you can drink Benskins Beer, among others, and eat very well in the restaurant section both at lunchtime and in the evening (not Sun). **B L D. £.**

Star Tavern   5 J 14
6 Belgrave Mews West SW1. 01-235 3019. *Fuller, Smith and Turner.* Small, friendly and traditional with open fires in both bars and some old Fullers brewery plaques. Sentimental doggie paintings in the downstairs bar. You might glimpse a famous TV face or two downstairs across the lunchtime dish of the day. **B.**

Tattersall's Tavern   2 H 13
Knightsbridge Green SW1. 01-584 7122. *Watneys.* Built on the former site of Tattersall's auction rooms this pub preserves the memory of their long association with racing. The bar has pictures of famous horses and race meetings, and there is a replica of the Tattersall Yard pump – the original of which is in the paddock at Newmarket. Tatters candlelit wine bar offers 'never-ending steaks', succulent seafood pancakes and good puds. **B L D.** *Wine bar closed Sat lunch and Sun.* **£** or **££.**

Turks Head   5 J 14
10 Motcomb St SW1. 01-235 2514. *Charrington.* Fancy Victorian setting with lots of atmosphere. Specially popular in winter when the open fire builds up a good fug in the bar. **B.**

MARYLEBONE ━━━━━━━━━

W1, NW1. Bounded west and east by Edgware Road and Great Portland Street, on the south by Oxford Street, and at the north by Regents Park and St John's Wood Road. That Marylebone was designed as a residential area is obvious from its attractive and sometimes imposing squares. Cutting north-south through the area is Baker Street where the best-known fictitious detective of them all, Sherlock Holmes, was supposed to have roomed with the amiable Dr Watson. More doctors further east in Harley Street, where the expensive specialists have their consulting rooms. Nearby is Wigmore Street with its concert hall where, by tradition, musicians make their London debut. The intensely bustling Oxford Street is internationally known for its shops, especially department stores and shoe shops. An important central artery of the area is Marylebone High Street with its chic boutiques, classy food stores and Continental-style cafes. Broadcasting House, which has been compared to a beached ocean liner, is the HQ of the BBC and stands at the bottom of Portland Place.

Tubes: Marble Arch, Edgware Road, Oxford Circus, Bond Street, Warren Street, Great Portland Street, Regents Park, Baker Street.

Allsop Arms   2 A 18
137 Gloucester Pl NW1. 01-723 5864. *Watneys.* Big, amiable, motherly pub with Webster's Yorkshire Bitter and Ruddles County on tap and good food, in a separate section, served at every session. Benches and tables on the wide pavement for fair weather drinking. **B.**

The Angel   2 E 19
37 Thayer St W1. 01-486 7763. *Samuel Smith.* Highly decorative Victorian pub with bars on two levels and picnic-site, bench-tables outside. Appropriate place to drink before or after a visit to the Wallace Collection in Manchester Square. Good hot and cold lunches available. **B.**

Baker and Oven   2 C 19
10 Paddington St W1. 01-935 5072. *Free House.* Small colourful orange and green pub with cosy basement restaurant. Traditional roasts and mouth-watering pies from 100-year-old baker's ovens. White-washed wine bar with black beams, quarry-tiled floor and pine furnishings is open at lunchtime only. Priv rm. **B L D** *(Reserve). Pub closed Sun.* **££.**

Beehive   **2 B 16**
7 Homer St W1. 01-262 6581. *Whitbread*. Until about
100 years ago this whole area was an apiary, producing
honey for the breakfast tables of London, which
explains the name of this small, friendly local.
Festooned with brass, and the pewter tankards of its
regulars hang behind the bar. Lots of darts, shove
ha'penny and cribbage played here. **B.**

Beehive   **2 C 17**
126 Crawford St W1. 01-935 9609. *Watneys*. And
here's another. Wood-panelling, tapestry seats and
pictures of old Marylebone. No bees. Pub grub at
lunchtime and in the evening. **B.**

Coach Makers Arms   **2 E 19**
88 Marylebone Lane W1. 01-935 9311. *Charrington*.
Popular with doctors, solicitors and tourists and well
known for its good food, available all the time. Lounge
bar has pictures of coaches and also, slightly
incongruously, of race horses. Large room with bar
upstairs. **B. £.**

Dover Castle   **2 D 20**
43 Weymouth Mews W1. 01-636 9248. *Watneys*.
Originally an 18th-century pub of many bars. Now
they've all been run into one but there are still strip
mirrors in the ceiling so the coachman, drinking in one
bar, could note when his employers finished their
drinks, in another bar, and beat them to the coach
door. Really good food served in a separate eating
room where children are welcome. Seats outside in the
mews when fine. Priv rm. **B.**

Duke of York   **2 C 16**
45 Harrowby St W1. 01-723 2914. *Charrington*. A
rugby, cricket and hockey enthusiasts' pub, proud
of its collection of ceramic figures of famous personalities, sporting and other. Tables and chairs outside
among the potted plants and window boxes. Good hot
and cold buffet. **B.**

The George   **2 E 21**
55 Great Portland St W1. 01-636 0863. *Free House*.
Good, popular Victorian pub, always packed with

people from the nearby BBC. Two bars – the George and the Glue Pot. The latter was so christened by Sir Henry Wood when he was conducting at Queen's Hall (destroyed in the war) because his orchestra tended to be late back from a visit to this, their local. There are usually savoury pies on offer – the steak and kidney is very good.**B.**

Horse and Groom   **2** E 21
128 Great Portland St W1. 01-580 4726. *Taylor Walker.* Plushy Victorian mews tavern with popular barmaids. Plenty of nice glass, pictures and bric-à-brac. Scoops in the rag trade at lunchtime and a generally younger crowd in the evening. Priv rm. **B.**

Marquis of Anglesea   **2** A 16
77 Ashmill St NW1. 01-723 7873. *Charles Wells.* Very Victorian atmosphere. Gas lit, though with some electrical support. Darts at one end of the big horse-shoe bar – all the rest is carpeted and comfortable. Hot and cold food available most of the time. **B.**

Pontefract Castle   **2** E 19
Wigmore St W1. 01-486 3551. *Free House.* Exuberant free house with several real ales, 20 malt whiskies and a flourish of flowery painting outside. Antiques, sea-chests, pictures from Pears Annual and Victorian porn inside. **B.**

Prince Regent   **2** D 19
71 Marylebone High St W1. 01-935 2018. *Charrington.* Strong Regency flavour here, with three torch-bearing blackamoor statues on the bar counter, letters from the Prince Regent and Mrs Fitzherbert on display and period caricatures. Rather popular with the BBC. Grill restaurant upstairs. Priv rm. **B L D** *(Reserve).* **££.**

The Worcester Arms   **2** D 17
89 George St W1. 01-935 6050. *Free House.* Very small, traditional pub with an intimate mock-Regency decor and lots of faithful regulars. There are always five real ales on the go, which vary with demand, and a 'guest beer of the week' which will oust one of the others if it goes down well. A drinker's pub, but quite smart for all that! **B.**

MAYFAIR

W1. Bounded by Piccadilly, Regent Street, Oxford Street and Park Lane. The name comes from the Fair that was held here every May for many years, and whose site is still marked by a plaque. This is a classy, fashionable area of London, although some of the elegant older buildings have been dwarfed by modern ones, even in Berkeley Square where the nightingale sang. That other famous Square, Grosvenor, is dominated by the huge American Embassy, sitting underneath its fierce bronze eagle. Mayfair is where most of the smart hotels stand – the May Fair itself, Claridges, The Dorchester, the Hilton and the Ritz just the other side of Piccadilly. Mayfair is also where you go for the Royal Academy, The Museum of Mankind, and Sotheby's, as well as for shops selling expensive clothes and jewellery, Persian rugs and paintings. Lending extra colour to the area is Shepherd Market, a little village with narrow streets and tiny houses that almost looks as though it's been dropped in by mistake, but in fact could be said to have started the whole thing – with its annual May Fair!

Tubes: Green Park, Hyde Park Corner, Marble Arch, Bond Street.

Argyll Arms   **2** G 20
18 Argyll St W1. 01-734 6117. *Free House.* Large, glamorous 300-year-old pub. The four downstairs bars and one upstairs bar glitter with magnificent mirrors and decorated glass, set in genuine mahogany, beneath Victorian plasterwork ceilings. Serves six real ales. Good selection of wines in the Palladium Bar, and hot meals lunchtime and evening Mon to Sat. **B.**

Audley   **2** G 17
41 Mount St W1. 01-499 1843. *Semi-Free House.* Pleasant Victorian pub, very popular with tourists. Upstairs, an English restaurant for fish and chips and apple pie. On the ground floor, three real ales and a carvery where a pair of formally clad chefs do the honours. **B L D. ££.**

Bunch of Grapes   **2** F 19
11 Dering St W1. 01-629 0531. *Whitbread.* Pretty,
wooden-fronted building with hanging baskets, tucked
away off Oxford Street. Olde-worlde red and gold
interior, hand pumps, and a liberal scattering of wine
labels. Almost a business man's club, with plenty of
regulars – and the few tourists who have left the beaten
track to find it. **B.** *Pub closed Sun.*

Bunch of Grapes   **2** I 17
16 Shepherd Market W1. 01-629 4989. *Free House.*
Built in 1882, on an old pub site, with traditional
Victorian interior and the flavour of a village local.
Upstairs there is a lunchtime restaurant to delight the
hearts of the greedy – pay a set price and help yourself
to as much food as you want. Priv rm. **B L.** *Closed* L *Sat
& Sun.* **£.**

Burlington Bertie   **2** H 19
21 Old Burlington St W1. 01-437 8355. *Charrington.*
Traditional, smartly redecorated pub with pictures on
its walls of the famous music-hall stars who sang about
Burlington Bertie, famous for rising at *10.30.* Quiet
juke-box, IPA, and lots of workers from the nearby
offices and hotels. Good hot and cold food. **B.** *Pub
closed Sat eve and all Sun.*

Chesterfield   **2** I 17
7 Shepherd St W1. 01-629 3645. *Charrington.* Bass,
American beers, lagers and wines are all on offer, but
this is an eater's pub, too, with an extensive and
impressive buffet at all times and a well-thought-of
traditional English restaurant above. **B L D. £** or **££.**

Guinea (Ye Old One Pound One)   **2** H 18
30 Bruton P1 W1. 01-409 1728. *Youngs.* Hidden away
in a narrow Mayfair Mews and dating back to 1423.
Original name probably suggested by a cattle pound
which is thought to have stood nearby when the whole
area was farmland. Guinea added in the reign of
Charles II when these gold coins were first minted.
Good but pricey dining room favours display cabinet
rather than menu. Famous for steak, Scotch salmon
and out of season fare. Clientele ranges from pop stars

to politicians but never includes the impecunious. **B L D** *(Reserve). Closed* **L D** *Sun,* **L** *Sat. Pub closed Sun.* **£££+.**

The Red Lion

Red Lion 2 H 17
Waverton St W1. 01-499 1307. *Watneys.* Lovely 17th-century Mayfair inn with forecourt for summertime drinking. Subdued old interior with pictures and prints of London, including a copy of a Canaletto. Restaurant serves English food with a French accent – interesting starters, Scotch beef for the steaks and a good cheeseboard. Mingle with models, actors and young businessmen. **B L D** *(Reserve).* **£££.**

Rose and Crown 2 I 16
2 Old Park Lane W1. 01-499 1980. *Free House.* Said to be one of the most haunted pubs in London because the doomed, en route for Tyburn, were sometimes incarcerated overnight in the cellars and apparently returned, in spirit only, later. Colourful and comfortable these days, with hot and cold meals over the bar twice a day (not Sun eve) and real ales. **B.**

Pub sign of London's only Running Footman

Running Footman   **2** H 17
5 Charles St W1. 01-499 2988. *Watneys*. Pub whose full
name was once the longest in London – 'I am the only
Running Footman'. A plaque on the wall explains the
task of these footmen – to run before a carriage
clearing the way and paying the tolls. Victorian decor,
housing four real ales. Popular with hotel staff and
croupiers from the nearby clubs. A la carte restaurant
upstairs serves traditional English food. **B L D.** *Closed
L Sat.* **£** or **£££.**

Shepherd's Tavern   **2** I 16
50 Hertford St W1. 01-499 3017. *Watneys*.
Bow-windowed pub, panelled in Canadian pine, and
much-favoured by the RAF during World War II.
Downstairs there are real ales and bar snacks. Upstairs
an à la carte restaurant serves English and French food
at lunchtime and in the evening every day. Don't miss
the public telephone installed in the Duke of
Cumberland's old sedan chair. **B L D.** **£** or **£££.**

PADDINGTON & BAYSWATER

W2, W9. Between Bayswater Road, Edgware Road and Queensway. Both areas are characterised by large Victorian buildings. Paddington itself varies from the slightly grubby area around the huge station, which was built by Brunel, to the enchanting area known as Little Venice where the Grand Union Canal reflects the tall plane trees along its towpath.

Bayswater Road runs alongside Kensington Gardens and Hyde Park. On a Sunday the park railings are hung with the paintings of amateur artists, who each book a specific patch in the hope of attracting buyers. At the corner of the Park near Marble Arch controversial views are voiced and argued with at Speaker's Corner. Queensway – a road that never sleeps – is dotted with small restaurants, patisseries and clothes shops. No use trying to read a newspaper over someone's shoulder here – it's unlikely to be in English.

Tubes: Lancaster Gate, Queensway, Bayswater, Paddington, Edgware Road.

Archery Tavern   2 C 13
4 Bathurst St W2. 01-402 4916. *Free House*. At the beginning of the 19th century archery became fashionable in Bayswater, and the tavern commemorates this revival by covering its walls with archery prints. You can't actually shoot an arrow, but you may throw a dart in the back room. **B.**

King's Head   1 A 10
33 Moscow Rd W2. 01-229 4233. *Truman*. Quietly traditional with a very good chess team, Truman's Best on draught and casseroles and quiches at lunchtime. In the evening they'll do you a sandwich – 'toasted, roasted or incinerated'. Occasional jazz on a Tue night. **B.**

Mitre   2 C 12
24 Craven Ter W2. 01-262 5240. *Whitbread*. Victorian pub with two ground floor bars and a cellar wine bar

called Moriarty's which has an appealingly creepy atmosphere, assisted by the fact that the ghost of an old coachman inhabits the part of the cellar that used to be the stables. Pub food at every session, from roast beef through to salads and sandwiches, and the usual quiche and pâté in the wine bar. Priv rm. **B.**

Paddington Stop
54 Formosa St W9. 01-286 6776. *Whitbread*. Newish pub in Little Venice, with a patio overlooking the canal. Sit outside on wooden benches and watch the barges pass by. On fine weekends there may be a barbecue. **B.**

Prince Alfred   **1 A 11**
112 Queensway W2. 01-229 1474. *Courage*. A crowded, cosmopolitan tourists' favourite with home-cooked lunches. Director's Bitter, and cheery background music. **B.**

Sussex   **2 B 13**
21 London St W2. 01-402 9602. *Taylor Walker*. Very handy for Paddington Station – in fact the pub and station are about the same age. Extraordinary ceiling that looks as if it's solidly mounted with brass door-knobs. Hot and cold meals served Mon to Sat. **B.**

Warwick Castle
6 Warwick Pl W9. 01-286 9604. *Charrington*. Regency pub in Little Venice looking out on to the Clifton Nurseries at the back. Wood-panelled walls, a wood block floor, an open fire and lots of prints of the old canal system to look at. **B.**

RICHMOND & KEW _____

Surrey. Richmond is a pleasant riverside town with a rural air about it. The Thames here flows between green banks and fields. Ducks dabble and herons fish. In the 2,000 acre Richmond Park, herds of dappled deer live wild, squirrels drop half-chewed acorns on

early-morning joggers, grown-ups ride horses and
children sail boats on the ponds. The Isabella
Plantation, in the heart of the Park, is a magic garden
of high trees, tiny waterfalls and bridges. There is
cricket on Richmond Green, which is overlooked by
Richmond Theatre, and a series of little streets full of
antique shops which rival The Lanes at Brighton.
There is also Richmond Hill with its expensive houses
and stunning views.

Kew is best known for its famous Royal Botanic
Gardens, with their beautiful trees and shrubs and
glittering Victorian glasshouses full of exotic plants
and ferns. The river here is appealing enough to have
inspired Camille Pissarro to paint it several times. For
waterside pubs, see **Riverside** section.

Tubes: Kew Gardens, Richmond.

Coach and Horses
8 The Green, Kew. 01-940 1208. *Youngs*. Big, old
coaching inn, redecorated in suitable style with
panelled walls, exposed beams, benches and
wheel-back chairs. Tables and chairs on the forecourt
give a good view of Kew Green and the cricket. Large
rose garden and patio at the back. Familiar European
food in the restaurant – kebabs, chicken Kiev, etc. **B L**
(Reserve). **££.**

Cricketers
The Green, Richmond. 01-940 4372. *Charrington*.
Victorian gabled building replacing an older one which
was burnt down in 1844. Lots of cricketing pictures at
the back to echo the cricket on the Green in front
(Richmond Green this time!). Upstairs there is a busy
wine bar with an à la carte International
(predominantly French) restaurant. **B L D. £** or **££.**

Greyhound
82 Kew Green, Kew. 01-940 0071. *Courage*. Tiny,
family pub, with a mock Tudor exterior and an
imitation olde-worlde interior, that attracts a mixed
crowd. Consult the pictures on the walls for the history
of old Kew. **B.**

Old Ship
3 King St, Richmond. 01-940 5014. *Youngs*. Very
shippy interior with dark panelling to set off the brass
trappings, lifebelts and anchors. Niches in the walls
house the model boats. Built as an inn at the beginning
of the 18th century – expanded to swallow up the next
door greengrocer at the end of the century – and now
serving hot snacks and good beer daily to a large and
varied crowd. Priv rm. **B.**

Princes Head
28 The Green, Richmond. 01-940 1572. *Fuller, Smith
and Turner*. Original building dates back to about 1740
– a few changes have been made but there is still a low,
beamed ceiling and some wood-panelling. Had a bad
reputation at one time. The oldest regulars still mutter
about the women of ill-repute who used to congregate
in the Ladies Bar – now amalgamated with the other
small bars into a single U-shape. Snacks at lunchtime
and in the evening. **B.**

Red Cow
59 Sheen Rd, Richmond. 01-940 2511. *Youngs*.
Cheery, sporty pub. The public bar has darts, shove
ha'penny and a Sunday sing-song when customers
bring guitars and other portable musical instruments.
Every so often the saloon plays the public at darts.
Very much a 'local'. **B.**

Roebuck
Richmond Hill, Richmond. 01-948 2329. *Youngers*.
Has been in business for over 200 years. The large
ground floor bar is divided into sections, all dark wood
beams and prints of old Richmond. Magnificent views
of the Thames valley. **B.**

White Swan
Old Palace Lane, Richmond. 01-940 0959. *Courage*.
Licensed by Royal Charter, so the swan wears a
coronet! Built about 400 years ago, at the end of a
terrace of cottages, to cheer the soldiers at the old
Sheen Barracks. Small walled garden. A range of hot
and cold food at lunchtime, plus a selection of cold
food in the evenings. Priv rm. **B.**

ST JOHN'S WOOD & REGENTS PARK

NW1, NW8. Between St John's Wood and Marylebone Stations and including the Park and Primrose Hill. Regents Park is one of London's most satisfying open spaces. It has a cricket ground, a bandstand, a lake and an open-air theatre, as well as lovely gardens and tree-lined walks. It was designed for the Prince Regent at the beginning of the 19th century by John Nash. At the northern end of the Park stands the Zoo, said to house the most varied selection of creatures of any zoo in the world. North of the Park is Primrose Hill with its lovely views – if you can fight your way to the top through the kites and model gliders, mostly flown by adults. The elegant residential area of St John's Wood is probably best-known for Lord's Cricket Ground, home of the MCC, the premier cricket club in Britain.

Tubes: Regents Park, Great Portland Street, St John's Wood, Marylebone.

The Clifton
96 Clifton Hill NW8. 01-624 5233. *Taylor Walker.* Discreetly sheltered in a leafy street with a delightful patio forecourt for alfresco drinking. Inside, all is Edwardiana and appropriately so, for here in the snug is where Edward VII and Lillie Langtry used to rendezvous. Three drinking areas served by an impressive, carved oak bar, and a new conservatory out at the back where you can enjoy good, varied pub food at lunchtime and in the evening. Prints of Lillie and the wayward King, china plates, stripped wood and three fireplaces give the pub a homely atmosphere and only one fruit machine detracts from the yester-year ambience. Imaginative and varied bar meals at every session. A choice of wines, as well as the regular spirits, beers and lagers. **B.**

Crockers
24 Aberdeen Pl NW8. 01-286 6608. *Vaux Free House.* Used to be called Crocker's Folly because Frank

Crocker built it on the mistaken assumption that Marylebone Station, with all its thirsty commuters, was about to be built nearby. Like all good follies it is extremely elaborate, with ornate flourishes on the ceiling, marble bar, pillars and fireplace. Real ale, snacks any time, and sometimes a pianist. **B.**

Knights of St John

7 Queen's Ter NW8. 01-586 5239. *Charles Wells*. Small and attractive and full of character. Recently acquired by the small Bedfordshire brewery whose Eagle and Bombardier Bitters are going down well. Good lunches, from sandwiches to dish of the day. **B.**

Ordnance Arms

29 Ordnance Hill NW8. 01-722 6143. *Charrington*. Built 300 years ago, in the middle of fields, as private army quarters. The fields and the military have gone leaving a very classy pub, with conservatory, garden and regular summer barbecues. Appeals to the England Cricket Team, the nearby recording studios and the well-heeled locals. **B.**

Rossetti

23 Queen's Grove NW8. 01-722 7141. *Fuller, Smith and Turner*. Large airy pub-trattoria with Rossetti etchings on the walls. Pub is on ground floor – very spacious and elegant with mirrors, plants, statues, good beers and wrought iron furniture on the patio. Restaurant is above and serves good Italian food. A varied menu with very wide price range. **B L D** *(Reserve)*. **££.**

SOHO & LEICESTER SQUARE

W1, WC2. Surrounded by Regent Street, Oxford Street, Charing Cross Road and Shaftesbury Avenue. This is London's oldest 'foreign quarter' with a high concentration of foreign restaurants, delicatessens and patisseries. It is bordered by London's theatreland and the major West End cinemas, and encompasses the whole of Chinatown. In winter a paper dragon roams the crowded streets proclaiming the Chinese New Year. In summer the Soho Festival offers live family entertainment and heavy betting on the Waiters' Race. All year round Berwick Street Market offers the cheapest fruit, vegetables and clothes in the West End. The Soho Society struggles on to preserve the village-like character of the place and seems to be winning in its attempts to turn back the tides of erotica and space-invader machines. However, sex and sleaze is still here with live strip shows and extravaganzas, blue movies, peep shows, dirty bookshops, lighted doorbells inviting you to call on a 'young model', and shops selling sex aids for DIY enthusiasts. This was once a hunting ground of a rather different nature, and 'So-ho' was the rallying cry of the huntsmen.

Tubes: Piccadilly Circus, Leicester Square, Tottenham Court Road.

Blue Posts   2 I 21
28 Rupert St W1. 01-437 1415. *Whitbread.* A 1900 reconstruction, with a mock Georgian façade, on the fringes of Soho. Saloon bar on the ground floor and lounge bar on the first, both decorated with original oil paintings and crowded with tourists, office workers and pre-theatre drinkers. Specialities are cocktails (see list on wall) and Irish coffee, but you will not be frowned at if you ask for ordinary coffee, tea, or even a glass of milk. Home-cooked food. **B.** *Pub closed Sun daytime.*

Coach and Horses   2 G 20
1 Great Marlborough St W1. 01-437 3282. *Whitbread.* Mid-18th-century coaching inn on what was once the road to Bath. You can sit outside in summer on pavement benches. There are four traditional ales including Flowers and Castle Eden. Upstairs wine bar for vino and food. **B.** *Pub closed Sun.*

Crown and Two Chairmen   2 H 22
31 Dean St W1. 01-437 8192. *Ind Coope.* Earned its name nearly 200 years ago by playing host to royalty who arrived by sedan chair – a crown carried by two

chairmen. You can drink real ale, branch out into cocktails, choose from a very wide range of hot and cold bar food and rub shoulders with writers, people from the film world and the odd TV actor. **B.**

Devonshire Arms   **2 I 21**
17 Denman St W1. 01-437 2445. *Free House.* Modernised old place with mock-Georgian dimpled windows. Main bar has dark oak furniture and sawdust on the floor. Spirits served straight from oak barrels and sherry from the wood. Four real ales and a choice of hot and cold food at every session. **B.**

Dog and Duck   **2 H 22**
18 Bateman St W1. 01-437 3478. *Ind Coope.* Built in 1773, and not updated, the Dog and Duck has one small bar, gleaming with polished wood and tiles and is often crowded with people from the worlds of film, publishing and jazz. There are always fresh flowers, as well as hot pies and sandwiches made by the landlord's wife. Burton Ale on handpumps. **B.**

Dog and Trumpet   **2 G 20**
38 Great Marlborough St W1. 01-437 5559. *Taylor Walker.* A brash, lively place at the beginning of Carnaby Street. Used to be called The Marlborough Head but changed to the Dog and Trumpet (symbol of HMV records) in memory of the 60s, when Carnaby Street swung far more than it does now and pop music found its dancing feet. Old (very pre-60s!) wind-up gramophones, and pictures of same, decorate the back bar. Juke-boxes in both ground floor bars and function room downstairs. **B.**

The French House (York Minster)   **2 H 22**
49 Dean St W1. 01-437 2799. *Watneys.* Small pub, with unremarkable decor, which was the London centre for the Free French during the war. De Gaulle drank here and so, in their day, did Brendan Behan and Dylan Thomas. Regulars come mostly from worlds of films, publishing and journalism and tend to drink more wine than beer. Champagne, pink or white, available in half bottles, and there's an excellent selection of French aperitifs. Tends to hide its charm from newcomers.

John Snow   2 H 21
39 Broadwick St W1. 01-437 1344. *Watneys*. Once the
Newcastle-on-Tyne. Took its new name when the
original John Snow, opposite, was demolished. The
man himself was a surgeon whose research into
waterborne disease helped rid Soho of an outbreak of
cholera in the early 19th century. The image of the
village water pump, source of all the trouble, is said to
reappear outside the pub from time to time – perhaps
to reassure customers that alcohol is best. Pool room
and bar upstairs.

Old Coffee House   2 H 20
49 Beak St W1. 01-437 2197. *Watneys*. Quite a few
London pubs began life as coffee houses in the 18th
century – this is one that chose not to change its name
when it ceased to serve the 'devil's brew', as coffee was
once called and went over to demon drink instead.
Long narrow panelled bar for civilised drinking.
Restaurant upstairs open Mon–Sat for good pub food.
This was the Soho Pub of the Year for 1987. **B L D. £.**

Red Lion   2 H 20
14 Kingly St W1. 01-734 4985. *Samuel Smith*.
Wood-panelled pub on two levels in a narrow Mayfair
street. There are open fires in winter, good lunches all
year round and a pleasant friendly atmosphere. **B.**

St James's Tavern   2 I 21
45 Great Windmill St W1. 01-437 5009. *Watneys*. Large
circular bar with gas lights, sawdusted floor and tiled
mural with scenes from Shakespeare's plays. Serves
full lunches, and early evening snacks. **B L. £.**

The Salisbury   5 J 22
90 St Martin's Lane WC2. 01-836 5863. *Ind Coope*.
Large Edwardian one-bar pub, glittering with cut glass
mirrors, gleaming with polished brass and glowing with
red plush. Excellent and reasonably priced hot and
cold food counter. The local for many of the nearby
theatres. **B.**

Store   2 H 20
15 Beak St W1. 01-734 5870. *Semi-Free House*. Began
life in the 17th century as a coffee house and became

the Cumberland Stores – probably a general and liquor
store – in the early 19th century. Nowadays it has the
look of an American bar with a solid wooden floor and
huge glass mirrors, two from the original stores.
Fosters and Yorkshire Bitter are on draught. There are
also 32 imported bottled beers and 164 spirits and
liqueurs. If you can't choose, try a cocktail. The
restaurant serves American food. Priv rm. **B L.** *Pub
closed Sat eve & all Sun.* **£.**

SOUTH EAST LONDON

SE1–SE25. This is the area south east of the River
Thames, beginning with Waterloo Station and the
South Bank Arts complex of National Theatre,
Hayward Gallery, Festival Hall and National Film
Theatre. It continues through Southwark with its fine
Gothic cathedral and ancient fruit and vegetable
market and on to Dulwich further south, with its lovely
park and village-like ambience.

Tubes: Waterloo, Elephant and Castle, New Cross.
Also British Rail from Charing Cross, London Bridge,
Victoria and Waterloo East.

Anerley Arms
Ridsdale Rd, Anerley SE20. 01-659 5552. *Samuel
Smith.* Once, pub and station stood entirely alone and
the local Scots landowner told the Railway Company
to call them 'Lonely'. His accent proved too much for
them and they christened the area 'Anerley' instead.
So in this case the pub, with its lovely mahogany
panelling, is truly the heart of the district. Real ale
from the wood and home-cooked lunches add to its
appeal. **B.**

Crown and Greyhound
73 Dulwich Village SE21. 01-693 2466. *Taylor Walker.*
Large turn of the century building housing three bars in

one, divided by arches and wrought iron. In summer there are usually weekend barbecues on the patio, and the swings in the garden are a delight to children. Try a candlelit dinner in the à la carte restaurant in the evening. The flourishing Bridge Club meets nightly. Priv rm. **B L D. £** or **££.**

Duke

125 Creek Rd SE8. 01-692 1081. *Whitbread.* Used to be The Duke of Marlborough but the name was truncated by common usage. Recent refurbishing didn't tamper with the Victorian engraved glass behind the bar. Always has live music on Fri and Sat – a mixture of folk, rock and roll and all sorts – in fact, The Flying Pickets started off here. Has a beer garden at the back and serves five real ales. Priv rm. **B.**

George Inn   **6 Q 27**

77 Borough High St SE1. 01-407 2056. *Whitbread.* London's only remaining galleried coaching inn, first mentioned in John Stow's 'History of London' in 1590 and rebuilt, after fire damage, in 1676. Patronised by

The George Inn

Dickens and featured in 'Little Dorrit'. There are two bars, real ale, a wine bar, and an à la carte restaurant. Offers a mix of olde Englishe entertainments – occasional performances of Shakespeare, adaptations of Chaucer, demonstrations of Medieval Knights in combat and, to ring the changes, Morris Dancing. Enquire for times. **B L D** *(Reserve)*. **££.**

Hercules Tavern   5 Q 22
2 Kennington Rd SE1. 01-928 6816. *Courage.* 19th century, with one bar done out in what can only be called mauve-with-cricketers – mauve velvet seating, mauve wallpaper and cricketing prints. Darts at one end, electronic games at the other. Priv rm. **B.**

King and Queen
Kimmeridge Rd, Mottingham SE9. 01-857 3492. *Truman.* Large and quite smart, with a pianist encouraging a sing-along in the saloon on Thur and Fri eves and Sun lunchtime. Bar snacks all week. Other delights include two pool tables, two snooker tables, three dart boards and a large garden. **B.**

Old Nun's Head
15 Nunhead Green SE15. 01-639 1745. *Charrington.* On the site of a nunnery destroyed during the Reformation. The Abbess was beheaded and her head set on a stake, which is why Nunhead Green is called what it is. Her ghost still haunts this comfortable wood-panelled pub with its real ale, quiet taped music and flourishing shove ha'penny teams. Hot and cold food at every session – grills a speciality. Priv rm. **B.** *Pub opens 19.00 Sat eve.*

The Warrior
185 Lower Rd, Rotherhithe SE16. 01-237 8902. *Charrington.* The Warrior was the first iron-clad battleship built for the Navy at nearby Deptford. This is a rebuilt version of an older pub which echoed the theme. Lounge bar done out like the lower deck of a man-of-war with port and starboard lights, nautical impedimenta and paintings, and portholes in the loos. On Sat, a group plays for the crowd – requests mostly. Full bar meals. **B.**

Wellington Tavern   **6 O 24**
81–83 Waterloo Rd SE1. 01-928 6083. *Free House*. Not surprisingly, the Wellington Tavern is decorated with murals of the Battle of Waterloo. Survivors of the daily Battle of Waterloo Station gather here to prepare themselves for the evening rush with a pint of real ale. There are six to choose from, and there's also a Carvery and a Wine Bar. Very handy for the Old Vic and South Bank complex. Enticing range of real ales: Arkells, Youngs, Burke's, Greene King and Godson's Black Horse. Priv rm. **B.**

SOUTH WEST LONDON

SW9–SW19. The area south west of the River Thames that stops short of Richmond and Kew to the west. This is an enormous area which incorporates some very different segments of South West London, each with its unique character. From Mortlake, where the Boat Race ends, through attractive Barnes with its village pond and ducks; through Putney where the Boat Race begins, and Wimbledon with its common and tennis connections; into industrial Wandsworth and Battersea, the latter with its landmark of a power station, which looks a bit like a vast Victorian dresser standing upside down; through Clapham, also renowned for its sprawling common and Brixton with its sometimes uneasy black community; and on out to the suburban areas of Tooting and Streatham.

Tubes: Northern, Victoria and District line stations to south of the River Thames. Also British Rail from Waterloo and Victoria.

Atlantic
389 Coldharbour Lane, Brixton SW9. 01-274 2832. *Ind Coope*. Rollicking West Indian pub, with plenty of enthusiastic regulars and an electric atmosphere,

housed in a listed building. Two main bars with a games room for darts, pool and dominoes. Sound system pumps reggae and soul into every corner.

Bedford
77 Bedford Hill, Balham SW12. 01-673 1756. *Watneys.* Old and interesting building with a balconied dome at one end. Used to be a Coroner's Court and is still haunted by one Dr James Gully, wrongly convicted in what is now the lounge. Good bar lunches. Members-only club upstairs has seven snooker tables. Priv rm. **B.**

The Brewery Tap
68 Wandsworth High St SW18. 01-870 2894. *Youngs.* The beer has to be good in this nice old pubby pub. It's attached to Youngs famous brewery – with its real ale, dray horses, and geese in the backyard – and the regulars are brewery staff and grooms. Meet the Youngs Ram and Gertie the Goat, who are tied up outside at the back every Sun. Eat in the restaurant upstairs, or choose from the comprehensive selection of bar snacks. Priv rm. **B L** *(Reserve). Closed* **L** *Sat & Sun.* **££.**

Bricklayer's Arms (The Brick)
32 Waterman St, Putney SW15. 01-788 1673. *Watneys.* J-shaped bar hung about with intriguing junk shop items, as though the contents of the attic had fallen through the ceiling. Quite a yuppy place these days. Open fire for winter and patio for summer. Home-cooked lunches Mon–Fri. **B.**

Charlie Butler
40 High St, Mortlake SW14. 01-878 2310. *Youngs.* Names for the man who was head horse-keeper at Youngs brewery for 43 years. Lots of photographs of amiable dray horses and one of the man himself driving his favourite. Friendly and sporty with three darts teams and a snooker team. Thames Bank United Football Club operates from here. You can sit outside, but the only view is of Watney's Brewery! **B.**

Cock Tavern   1 F   2
360 North End Rd SW6. 01-385 6021. *Trumans.*

Friendly, spacious, nicely decorated one-bar pub offering traditional English meals at every session. **B.**

Fox and Grapes
Camp Rd, Wimbledon Common SW19. 01-946 5599. *Courage.* Julius Caesar camped near here – hence 'Camp Road' and the downstairs 'Caesar Bar' – which is 300 years old. Rambling family pub, right on the common, with Dickens characters peering out from the panelling and impressive lunches (not Sun). **B.**

Hand in Hand
6 Crooked Billet, Wimbledon Common SW19. 01-946 5720. *Youngs.* Jolly and young, with a family room in an annexe. Lovely little patio in front with a tree and plants. Lino and wooden benches in the larger, more old-fashioned half of the bar – carpets and wrought-iron round the other side. Bar snacks are always available and the upstairs restaurant opens from Mon to Fri at lunchtime to serve steaks, duck à l'orange and various puds. **B L. £ or ££.**

Leigham Arms
1 Wellfield Rd, Streatham SW16. 01-769 6117. *Charrington.* Ale has been served on this site since the 16th century. Public bar always crowded with real ale enthusiasts – small snug and lounge for slightly quieter drinking. **B.**

Leo's   4 L   4
490 Fulham Rd SW6. 01-385 3942. *Watneys.* One-time music pub which has become an 'open house' theme pub. Lots of red and grey woodwork, a video jukebox and pleasant food. Has been the Red Lion and the New Golden Lion. The peeved expression on the face of the leonine effigy on the roof may be due to the fact that he is not strictly all there. **B.**

Maltese Cat
Aubyn Sq, Roehampton SW15. 01-876 7534. *Youngs.* Roehampton used to be a polo-playing area so the pub has been named after the polo pony in Kipling's well-known story. Huge garden and patio, floodlit at night, reached through French windows from saloon. A juke-

box has been installed, on request, but the volume is reasonably discreet. Live music Thur and Sun evenings. The local for the nearby hospital and college. **B.**

Pied Bull

498 Streatham High Rd SW16. 01-764 4003. *Youngs.* Nowadays the bull himself is a ceramic image on the outside wall – once he probably snorted on Streatham Common, opposite. Not that the common is dull now – in season, there is cricket, football and visiting circuses. Inside the pub – five friendly Victorian bars where you can eat snacks anytime and drink real ale. **B.**

Plough

42 Christ Church Rd, East Sheen SW14. 01-876 7833. *Watneys.* About 100 years ago, three Queen Anne cottages were knocked into one to make an attractive wood-beamed pub with lots of nooks and crannies and country-antique-shop bric-a-brac. Very busy – mostly with regulars because it isn't easy to find unless you know it's there. If you do find it, you can stay the night – there's accommodation with its own bathroom. **B.**

Red Lion

2 Castlenau, Barnes SW13. 01-748 2984. *Fuller, Smith and Turner.* Open fires to warm you in winter and, in summer, a large grassy garden with swings and slides for the children; and a patio with tables and chairs for the grown-ups. Barbecues are held on fine weekends in summer. Usually, there are famous faces to be spotted among the regular families. **B.**

Rose and Crown

55 High St, Wimbledon SW19. 01-947 4713. *Youngs.* Well-restored 17th-century pub where Swinburne once drank. Popular with families and the Wimbledon Rugby Club. Children are welcome to eat in the Buttery Bar and to play in the large paved garden at the back of the ivy-covered building. **B.**

Sun Inn

7 Church Rd, Barnes SW13. 01-876 5893. *Taylor Walker.* Famous, crowded, and popular with the

The Sun Inn

young. Rebuilt in 1750 on an old pub site, opposite Barnes Pond with its trees, lush rushes and ducks. Country atmosphere, with oak, brasses, cane-backed chairs and highly acclaimed sandwiches. **B.**

STRAND & FLEET STREET

WC2, EC4. From Charing Cross Station to Ludgate Circus. The character of Fleet Street is changing as the offices and printing works of the national newspapers begin to move out, yet the name will probably remain synonymous with 'the press' for a long time to come. This is an intriguing area of concealed alleys and courts with the River Fleet flowing through a conduit beneath. When Fleet Street leaves the City, past the two dragon guardians, and becomes the Strand it enters the world of the law because all around are the four Inns of Court – Middle and Inner Temple, Lincoln's Inn and Gray's

Inn. The Royal Courts of Justice, more usually called
the Law Courts, which front on to the Strand itself,
unite all four Inns. At lunchtime and in the early
evening, most of the nearby pubs are well stocked
with barristers and journalists. By about *21.00*, the
'wigs and pens' have departed and some of the pubs
close their doors. *Note that several are closed for all or
part of the weekend.*

Tubes: Charing Cross, Strand, Aldwych, Temple,
Chancery Lane, Blackfriars.

Cartoonist   **6 K 27**
76 Shoe Lane EC4. 01-353 2828. *London Taverns.*
This is the headquarters of the International
Cartoonist Club and there are framed original
cartoons everywhere – all over the walls of the ground
floor bar, beside the wide, brass-railed stairway, and
all over the walls of the quieter downstairs bar. Many
of the regulars are pressmen who are used to the
decor. Newcomers read the walls. Home-cooked
snacks and meals. **B.** *Pub closed Sat & Sun.*

Cheshire Cheese, Ye Olde   **6 K 26**
145 Fleet St EC4. 01-353 6170. *Samuel Smith's.* A
somewhat rambling building with low ceiling'd

Ye Olde Cheshire Cheese

interior, three smallish bars and three small restaurants, all with oak tables and sawdusty floors. The 14th-century crypt of Whitefriars Monastery is still intact beneath the cellar bar and you can go and stare at it, or book it for a party. No snacks and only one bitter, (Samuel Smith's Old English Brew), but stout English cookery. Famous for good, rich game puddings in autumn and winter. A celebrity is always invited to cut the first pudding of the season in Oct. Priv rm. **L D** *(Reserve)*. *Pub open to 21.00. Closed Sat & Sun.* **££.**

Cheshire Cheese   **6** K 25
5 Little Essex St WC2. 01-836 2347. *Courage.* Intimate Jacobean pub with original beams and three bars. Go to the Millers Bar for wine, doubles, and good snacks, and coffee and biscuits in the mornings; to the saloon for real ale and the odd roll; down to the Dive Bar for bottled beers, spirits and hot lunches. Regulars come from the nearby law courts. Inhospitable ghost spends its nights moving an enormously heavy fruit machine across saloon bar door. **B.** *Pub closed Sat & Sun.*

Cock Tavern, Ye Olde   **6** K 26
22 Fleet St EC4. 01-353 8570. *Truman.* Small but good tavern which used to stand in Apollo Court but crossed the road towards the end of the 19th century to make way for a new building. Nell Gwynn, Pepys, Goldsmith, Sheridan and Garrick once drank under the sign of the Cock – now you will find journalists and barristers. Dickensian mementoes line the walls. Large dining room specialises in puddings and pies, with a cold buffet in summer. Also, popular bar lunches. Priv rm. **B L** *(Reserve)*. *Closed Sat & Sun.* **££.**

Devereux   **6** K 25
20 Devereux Court WC2. 01-583 4562. *Courage.* First the town house of the Earl of Essex, then a coffee house, now a pub. The comfortable restaurant serves English food for up to 46 customers. Between *13.00–14.00* you are liable to be trampled underfoot by members of the legal profession and the judiciary

rushing to stoke up in the brief lunchtime recess from nearby Middle Temple. Priv rm. Accommodation. **B L** *(Reserve). Closed Sat & Sun.* **££.**

Edgar Wallace   **6 K 25**
40 Essex St WC2. 01-353 3120. *Whitbread.* Used to be called The Essex Head – in fact Dr Johnson founded The Essex Head Club here in 1783. Present decor inspired by the memory of the writer Edgar Wallace, with copies of his books, relevant pictures, and framed personal letters, mostly donated by his daughter. There is a good à la carte menu in the small restaurant upstairs. Priv rm. **B L.** *Pub closed Sat eve & all Sun.* **£.**

The George   **6 K 26**
213 The Strand WC2. 01-353 9238. *Charrington.* Fine old timbered inn opposite the Royal Courts of Justice. Though the sign shows George III, it's actually named after a more ordinary George who owned it when it was a coffee house. One long, beamed, cosy bar, with cold cabinet for snacks. Upstairs lunchtime restaurant is carvery style. Popular with the defence, the prosecution and tourists. Priv rm. **B L** *(Reserve). Closed* **L** *Sat & Sun. Pub closed Sat & Sun eves.* **££.**

Gilbert & Sullivan   **6 J 24**
23 Wellington St WC2. 01-836 6930. *Whitbread.* The original Gilbert & Sullivan, in John Adam Street, was damaged by fire in 1979 and so the photographs, playbills and musical scores of the operas were moved here, to what used to be The Old Bell. The Mikado Cocktail Lounge will serve you Gin Sling or a glass of wine. **B.**

Lyceum   **6 K 24**
354 Strand WC2. 01-836 7155. *Samuel Smith.* There's a peaceful tap room downstairs, a plant-filled conservatory on the ground floor, and an upstairs lounge with good views over the Strand. Real ale, good bar lunches – and a passage connecting the pub to what was the Lyceum Theatre, now a club and disco, where Sir Henry Irving once declaimed on stage. **B.**

Old Bell Tavern   **6** K 26
95 Fleet St EC4. 01-583 0070. *Free House.* Built by Sir Christopher Wren in 1670 to house and serve the workmen rebuilding nearby St Bride's Church, which had been destroyed in the Great Fire. Single U-shaped bar is made cosy with seating nooks, chairs and tables. Small, friendly and unpretentious. Five real ales are on draught. **B.** *Pub closed Sun.*

Poppinjay   **6** K 26
119 Fleet St EC4. 01-353 5356. *Charrington.* Cheerful modern pub next to the 'Daily Express' building. Full of journalists at lunchtime and printers hot from the press in the evening. As you go in the door, before you enter the bar, you are faced with a huge stone which used to hang over the entrance to Poppins Court. On it is carved a Poppinjay, emblem of the Abbots of Cirencester who once had a house here in which, rumour has it, a great deal of drinking went on. Some stuffed birds stand around the bar to pick up the theme. **B.** *Pub closed Sun eve.*

Printer's Devil   **6** K 26
98 Fetter Lane EC4. 01-242 2239. *Whitbread.* Takes its title from the traditional nickname for a printer's apprentice (though the sign shows a 'real' devil at a press). Upstairs Wine Bar is open weekday lunchtimes. Real live drinking printers complete the decor. **B L.** *Closed* **L** *Sat. Pub closed all Sun.* **£.**

Punch Tavern   **6** K 26
99 Fleet St EC4. 01-353 6658. *Charrington.* Punch magazine was conceived here in 1841. The choice of title was inspired by the Punch and Judy shows which in those days used to enliven nearby Ludgate Circus. The tavern changed its name in honour of the magazine and acquired a brass figure of Mr Punch (which has recently been pinched) and some original cartoons by way of relevant decor. Nice etched mirrors. **B.**

Seven Stars   **6** J 26
53 Carey St WC2. 01-242 8521. *Courage.* Behind the Law Courts stands this early 17th-century pub, one of

the smallest in London. One end of the bar is given over to a past customer – Charles Dickens – with caricatures of his characters. The other side is decorated with cartoons of judges. Full of barristers and pressmen drinking Director's Bitter and snatching a quick snack. *Pub closed Sat & Sun.* **B.**

Sherlock Holmes   **5** K 22
10 Northumberland St WC2. 01-930 2644. *Whitbread.*
A good starting point for a pub crawl down the Strand. Used to be the Northumberland Arms Hotel, which Sir Arthur Conan Doyle mentioned in 'The Hound of the Baskervilles'. In 1957 it changed its name and took the fictitious detective as its theme. Upstairs, next to the restaurant, is a perfect reconstruction of Holmes' study. Down in the bar are all manner of relevant cuttings and curios, including the head of the legendary hound and plaster casts of its huge feet (paws for effect!) **B L D** *(Reserve).*
Closed **L** *Sat,* **L D** *Sun.* **££.**

Ship and Shovel   **5** K 22
2 Craven Passage WC2. 01-930 7670. *Free House.* Just behind Charing Cross Station. When the Thames flowed past, and this was called The Ship, the dockers who drank here left their long shovels propped outside. So the name was extended. Even though the river has moved further away, the recent refit includes a large ship's wheel and portholes. Serves Ruddles, Brakspear's and Adnam's. **B.**

White Horse   **6** K 26
90 Fetter Lane EC4. 01-242 7846. *Friary Meux.*
Popular old coaching inn with two comfortable bars decorated with old prints, plates and brassware. Dining room upstairs is open at lunchtimes only and can serve you a sandwich, a seafood pancake, lobster, or dish of the day. Insomniac ghost in smart dress-coat rattles bottles in the cellar at night and occasionally makes himself an early morning cup of tea. Priv rm. **B L** *Mon–Fri.* **£.**

White Swan   **6** L 26
28/30 Tudor St EC4. 01-353 5596. *Truman.* Between

the Temple and the offices of the 'Daily Mail'. Not surprisingly, full of printers, reporters, solicitors and barristers. Recently smartened up, but still very much a local, with its own darts team. Affectionately known as the Mucky Duck. Hot snacks from Ben's Larder. **B.** *Pub closed Sat lunchtime.*

Witness Box   **6** L 26
36 Tudor St EC4. 01-353 6427. *Watneys.* Built in 1974 in the cellar of a modern office block, though the bar is decorated in authentic Edwardian style. A show-piece for crime reporters, with walls covered in cuttings on notable criminal events. The pub itself awards a plaque to the reporter whose crime story is voted best of the year. Very good food – everything freshly cooked on the premises. The upstairs wine bar does food too – anything from a snack to a full meal. **B.** *Pub closed Sat & Sun.*

VICTORIA & PIMLICO

SW1. Bounded by the Thames, Buckingham Palace Road, Buckingham Gate and Horseferry Road. Victoria is mostly to do with people coming and going. It is dominated by Victoria rail, coach and underground stations, which in turn accounts for the fact that many of the large old houses have been turned into small hotels to accommodate the new arrivals. The trucks and juggernauts that thunder down Vauxhall Bridge Road to cross the Thames for the south, and sometimes the Continent, all add to the general sense of movement, which can be stimulating or unsettling. Pimlico was mostly built in the 1850s. It is restless in a different way – with a high proportion of young people, in flats and bedsitters, and a plethora of restaurants, cafés, wine bars, market stalls, late night food shops and all night launderettes. It also has two key attractions: down by the Thames, on Millbank, stands the Tate Gallery, the home of the principal collection of British art and modern painting; and in the top corner of the area stands Buckingham Palace itself.

Tubes: Victoria, Pimlico.

The Albert   **5 M 17**
52 Victoria St SW1. 01-222 5577. *Watneys*. Grand, imposing Victorian pub positively gleaming with polished wood and fitted with original gas lights and engraved glass windows. Upstairs, past portraits of Prime Ministers is an excellent restaurant serving traditional English roasts and boasting an extensive wine list. Busy but efficient, this handsome pub is popular with MPs (there's a division bell in the restaurant) and is close to New Scotland Yard. Winner of the 1984 'Standard' Pub of the Year Award. **B L D** *(Reserve)*. **££.**

Barley Mow   **5 O 18**
104 Horseferry Rd SW1. 01-222 2330. *Watneys*. Westminster Hospital's local. Very pretty outside, with its red awnings, shrubs in tubs, and chairs on the pavement. Cosy inside with comfortable seating, copies of Hogarth prints, and an open fire in winter. Michelle's Restaurant is open weekday lunchtimes. Priv rm. **B L** *(Reserve)*. **££.**

Cask and Glass   **5 L 17**
39 Palace St SW1. 01-834 7630. *Watneys*. Tiny, busy, friendly 19th-century pub – a little like a dolls' house from outside, with its hanging baskets and troughs full of flowers, among which stand some tables and chairs. Very comfy and pleasant. Renowned for its sand-wiches. **B.**

Colonies   **5 L 17**
25 Wilfred St SW1. 01-834 1407. *Watneys*. Small pub converted about 1975 into a nostalgic corner for old colonials. You can drink surrounded by photographs of outposts of the lost Empire, the heads of stags and antelopes, and sundry spears and whips. Or go out the back on nice days. Popular with businessmen in the oil business. **B.**

Fox and Hounds   **5 M 12**
29 Passmore St SW1. 01-730 6367. *Charrington.* The
last in London without a spirit licence, this small,
gentle pub has been recently extended, although it is
still definitely on the intimate side. Dark wood
furniture, old prints, and quite a few regular dog
customers. Snacks Mon–Fri only, but they'll always
make you a toasted sandwich. **B.**

Lord High Admiral   **5 N 16**
43 Vauxhall Bridge Rd SW1. 01-828 3727. *Ind Coope.*
Fairly new pub replacing an older one of the same
name. Bare brick walls, wooden stalls with red leather
seating. Always full of young tourists. Tables out
front and a large green at the back (which belongs to
the nearby estate, but people do drink there).
Extensive lunch menu and snacks in the evening,
usually with chips or mash. **B.**

Morpeth Arms   **5 P 18**
58 Millbank SW1. 01-834 6442. *Youngs.* Comfortable
traditional pub near the Tate Gallery furnished in
Victorian style. Sit on the patio and watch, through
gaps in the traffic, as boats pass by. But don't go down
to the cellars which are connected to an old tunnel,
through which prisoners were once hustled en route
for the penal colonies – if you do, phantom water may
drip on your head and a phantom hand may tap you
on the shoulder. Hot and cold meals at every session.
B.

Orange Brewery   **5 M 12**
37 Pimlico Rd SW1. 01-730 5378. *Semi-Free House.*
Rumour has it that Nell Gwynn once sold oranges in
the square opposite and so suggested the name.
History has it that the pub has been in its time, a
coffee house and a tavern with a theatre. Has just
taken a welcome step back into the past, installing gas
lighting and a brewery in the cellar which produces a
regular ale called SW1 and a stronger version called
SW2. The pies are home-made, too. **B.**

Rising Sun   **5 N 13**
44 Ebury Bridge Rd SW1. 01-730 4088. *Youngs.*

Handy for Victoria rail and coach stations and so attracting a cosmopolitan crowd, plus the bands of the Guards. Sit out in front and watch the traffic, or go inside and admire the model boats, paintings of boats and decorative plates – some new, some genuine antiques. Full lunches. Priv rm. **B.**

St George's Tavern   **5** N 15
14 Belgrave Rd SW1. 01-834 4170. *Charrington.* Villagey Pimlico pub right on the edge of Belgravia, with a very congenial atmosphere. Real ale and a recently expanded food operation. **B.**

WEST LONDON ━━━━━━

W3–W6, W12–W14. Chiswick, Hammersmith, Shepherd's Bush, Ealing and Acton. Chiswick was a wealthy riverside village in the 18th century and the beautiful Georgian waterfront houses, with their climbing plants and flood barriers, stretch all the way to Hammersmith Mall. The Chiswick and Hammersmith waterfront pubs come under the '**Riverside pubs**' section. Inland Chiswick is also extremely attractive – here you will find the 17th century house that belonged to Hogarth and the small-scale Palladian appeal of Chiswick House in its lovely grounds. Hammersmith, which gives its name to a Disney-like Thames bridge, is firmly on the map of tourists and central Londoners because of its cinemas, dance halls (the old Hammersmith Palais was the most famous of them all) and the popular Riverside Studios with its exciting range of dance, drama, music and general arts facilities.
Shepherd's Bush is well-known for the BBC TV theatre, where audiences gather to watch programmes being recorded, and for two other important centres of entertainment – BBC TV Centre and the famous White City Stadium where many a good man has gone to the greyhounds.

Ealing and Acton are a complete mixture of tree-lined residential streets, suburban shops, and factories commited to various kinds of light industry.

Tubes: Hammersmith, Shepherd's Bush and points west on the District, Central and Metropolitan lines.

Baron's Court Tavern   1 F 1
Comeragh Rd W14. 01-385 4064. *Watneys.* The closest pub to Queen's Tennis Club – traditional, even elegant, with nice food six days a week, trad jazz on Mon eve and varied live music on a Thur eve. The landlord usually has some scheme on hand to raise money for charity. **B.**

Crown and Anchor
374 Chiswick High Rd W4. 01-995 2607. *Youngs.* There's been an inn on this site since the days when Turnham Green was the scene of a battle between the soldiers of Henry VII and the pretender to the throne. This is a drinking and talking pub (popular with the local football team). A carvery upstairs serves home-cooked English food. Priv rm. **B L D.** *Closed* **L D** *Sat*, **D** *Sun.* **£.**

Drayton Court
2 The Avenue, Ealing W13. 01-997 1019. *Fuller, Smith and Turner.* Known locally as Dracula's Castle because of its extravagantly turreted outline. Lounge bar decorated with the crests of local families, whose pennants hang from the ceiling. Garden at the back has a lawn that used to be a bowling green. Good beer. Priv rm. **B.**

Fox and Goose
Hanger Lane W5. 01-997 2441. *Fullers.* Large, traditional and smart, with oak-panelling, plants and a pretty garden for relaxing in. A good, solid pub, usually well-packed. Home-cooked bar food. Priv rm. **B. ££.**

Fox and Hounds and Mawson Arms
110 Chiswick Lane South W4. 01-994 2936. *Fullers.* A 300-year-old listed building, where Alexander Pope

Drayton Court

once lived, right beside Fuller's brewery. When the Mawson Arms opposite closed down, the Fox and Hounds preserved its title and became known as 'the pub with two names'. There are snacks at lunchtime, a pianist encouraging a sing-along on Fri, Sat & Sun eves. **B.**

Hand and Flower   **1 D 3**
1 Hammersmith Rd W14. 01-602 1000. *Courage.* Lively pub which goes in for speciality acts on Mon to Thur evenings – fire eaters, magicians, and other Barnum-style novelties. There is a resident DJ Mon – Sat, so that the customers can show off too, and the English restaurant is open whenever there is an

exhibition at Olympia opposite – in other words, nearly all the time. Priv rm. Accomodation. **B L D. ££.**

Haven Arms
Haven Lane W5. 01-997 0378. *Watneys*. 19th century, oak-beamed country pub that was used as a courthouse in its early days. Big old picture painted on the chimney breast shows a murderer flanked by two Peelers. Pretty paved beer garden recently did rather well in a local competition. **B.**

King's Head
214 High St, Acton W3. 01-992 0282. *Fullers*. Large yet intimate pub made very pretty with pictures on all the walls. Attractive garden for fine days. Good bar meals at every session, and jazz every Wed eve, alternating between trad and mainstream. Priv rm. **B.**

New Inn
62 St Mary's Rd W5. 01-840 4179. *Watneys*. It's tradition all the way in this old world pub with brick walls, wooden rafters and open fireplaces. A goodly selection of real ales: Websters, Ruddles, Mann's IPA and Combes. Wholesome English food served by wenches in traditional garb. Out the back, a huge secluded beer garden and open courtyard. **B.**

North Star
43 Ealing Broadway W5. 01-567 4848. *Ind Coope*. The North Star was an early steam engine, rather than a light in the sky. This large pub lightens the life of a rich variety of people in its three different bars. The front bar has a juke-box and a youngish crowd. The middle bar is for the hungry, offering anything from a roast to a ploughman's, Mon–Sat, lunchtime and evening; on Sun the odd dish of cockles keeps body and soul together. The small end bar, called the VIP lounge, is where you go for a quiet read of your paper over a Scotch. **B.**

Queen's Head   1 C 1
Brook Green, Hammersmith W6. 01-603 3174. *Watneys*. 300-year-old wayside inn. Dick Turpin is said to have hidden here many times. Beer garden at the

back and public tennis courts at the front. Goes in for food in a big way – not only in the steak restaurant but also in the permanent (including Sun), prize-winning home-made buffet. **B L D** *(Reserve)*. *Closed* **D** *Sun*, **L** *Sat*. **££.**

Red Lion and Pineapple
281 High St W3. 01-992 0465. *Fullers.* Huge public bar, with pool table and dart board. The garden bar has the greater part of a dead tree wedged between floor and ceiling and opens on to a real garden. Saloon leads into a small snug and also a restaurant. Decent English food with a special each day. **B L.** *Closed* **L** *Sun*. **£.**

Rose and Crown
Church Pl, St Mary's Rd W5. 01-567 2811. *Fullers.* Typical 1920s pub with a large, grassy garden and a good range of bar food to accompany the real ale – hot food, salads and sandwiches. Friendly place where people come for a drink and a yarn. **B.**

Rutland
Lower Mall, Hammersmith W6. 01-748 5586. *Watneys.* A good place to extend your knowledge of ale – guest beers come from all over the world – Japan, France, Australia. Hot snacks are available to accompany them if required. Mon is Curry Night, Thur is Jazz Night and there's a roast lunch on Sun. Priv rm. **B. L** *Sun.*

The Sutton Lane
12 Sutton Lane, Chiswick W4. 01-994 4107. *Watneys.* Recent refurbishing has brought the old 'Hole in the Wall' upmarket. It now has a Cocktail Bar, a Tap Room, and a Public Bar with pool table and dart board. Illuminated beer garden has a chess set carved in the ground – yes, there are chess pieces and yes, you may play with them. **B.**

Thatched House
115 Dalling Rd W6. 01-748 6174. *Youngs.* Thatched no more – though it used to be, in the days before the buildings opposite replaced the old orchard. Recently refurbished but traditional and much-loved by its regulars. **B.** *Pub open to 23.00 Mon–Sat.*

WESTMINSTER WHITEHALL & ST JAMES'S

SW1. Bordered by the Thames, Northumberland Avenue and Haymarket, Piccadilly, Buckingham Gate and Horseferry Road. This is an area rich in gardens, government and gentlemen's clubs. St James's Park and Green Park, divided only by The Mall, were acquired by Henry VIII in 1532. They offer good views of Buckingham Palace, the imposing sweep of Carlton Terrace, Whitehall and Westminster Abbey. The Mall and Constitution Hill are sometimes the scene of royal processions to and from the Palace, and Horseguards Parade is the setting for the annual ceremony of Trooping the Colour.

Down by the river stand the Houses of Parliament, seat of British Government, and conveniently close, just off Whitehall, you can find Nos 10 and 11 Downing Street – formal homes of the Prime Minister and the Chancellor of the Exchequer. St James's is dominated by St James's Palace, again built by Henry VIII, and still the official court to which foreign ambassadors are accredited.

Tubes: St James's Park, Westminster, Embankment, Piccadilly, Green Park.

Blue Posts   2 1 19
6 Bennet St SW1. 01-493 3350. *Watneys*. Charming traditional pub (Lord Byron used to live next door) with an original sedan chair. Upstairs, the old English Carving Room serves English roasts and treacle puds. **L D** *(Reserve). Pub closed Sat eve & Sun.* **££.**

Buckingham Arms   5 L 18
62 Petty France SW1. 01-222 3386. *Youngs*. Amiable mid-Victorian pub. The walls are hung with prints associated with the Duke of Buckingham. Gathering place for businessmen – especially on the pavement outside. **B.**

Clarence   **5** L 21
53 Whitehall SW1. 01-930 4808. *Free House*. There's a
preservation order on this 18th-century house with its
gaslights inside and out, sawdusted floor, wooden
pews and tables. Popular with Civil Servants from the
Ministries of Agriculture and Defence next door.
There are bar meals twice daily, six real ales, and a
regular 'guest' beer at a special cheap rate. As a
concession to the summertime tourists, a costumed
minstrel entertains. **B.**

Cockney Pride   **2** J 19
6 Jermyn St SW1. 01-930 5339. *Free House*. Nostalgic
reconstruction of a Victorian Cockney pub, where real
ale is served along with sausages and mash. Fairly quiet
at lunchtimes, and in the small bar in the evenings, but
rumbustious in the big bar every night with lively
cockney bands. Restaurant, called Cockney Bar, has a
separate entrance, a cocktail bar and a menu running
from burgers to steaks. **B L D. ££.**

Golden Lion   **5** J 19
25 King St SW1. 01-930 7227. *Ind Coope*. This is where
you go to recuperate when you've run yourself ragged
bidding for valuables at Christie's, opposite. Very
good food, particularly at lunchtime, and Burton Ale
and Best Bitter from hand pumps. Back cabinet of
downstairs bar is very old and considered rather
special. Priv rm. **B.** *Pub closed Sun.*

Old Star   **5** M 18
66 Broadway SW1. 01-222 8755. *Whitbread*. Used to
be nicknamed The Cab House when it was a regular
stopping-off point for drivers of horse-drawn hansoms
– and some present-day cabbies still call it that. On the
walls, prints of the pub and area. Around the bar,
drinkers from the Houses of Parliament, the Home
Office and New Scotland Yard. Downstairs the Crown
Vaults wine bar. Priv rm. **B.** *Pub closed Sat eve &
Sun.*

Red Lion   **5** J 19
23 Crown Pas SW1. 01-930 8067. *Watneys*. A villagey
pub, surrounded by small shops, on a site which once

supported a hospital for 'leprous maidens', and very near the site of the last duel fought on English soil. Home-cooked food at every session, and a lunchtime snack bar upstairs. Priv rm. **B.**

Red Lion   **5** J 20
2 Duke of York St SW1. 01-930 2030. *Ind Coope.* A little gem of a Victorian gin palace with rich mahogany panelling and beautifully preserved mirrors, each engraved with a different British flower. All glow and glitter inside – and usually so full that the pavement becomes an extension of the bar. Commodity and stock brokers gather here for the four traditional ales and the home-cooked food, served at every session. **B.**

Engraved mirror in Red Lion, Duke of York Street

Silver Cross   **5** L 21
33 Whitehall SW1. 01-930 8350. *Watneys*. 13th-century building with a preservation order on its fine Tudor waggon-vaulted ceiling. It was licensed as a brothel by Charles I and has been a tavern since 1674 – but no one has got around to revoking (or making use of) the brothel licence. Tudor maiden whose portrait is on the wall haunts the upper floor. Home-cooked lunches and hearty evening buffet in a pleasant and friendly atmosphere. **B.**

Tom Cribb   **5** J 21
36 Panton St SW1. 01-839 6536. *Charrington*. Named for the 17th-century fist fighter, who ran it in the days when it was the Union Tavern. Then it was a sporting pub, with cockfights in the cellar – now the haunt of businessmen and theatre-goers. Still remembers its past, with boxing prints around the walls. Made its film debut in 'Fanny by Gaslight'. **B.**

Westminster Arms   **5** M 19
9 Storeys Gate SW1. 01-222 8520. *Free House*. Big Ben Bar, downstairs, aims to be a typical English inn and serves several real ales. The Queen Anne Bar, upstairs, is for double measures, snacks and bottled beers. Storeys Wine Bar, which closes at *20.00*, has food hot and cold, wine chambrer or frais! **B.**

LIVE MUSIC PUBS ⸺⸺⸺

These vary enormously from pubs in which one pianist plays old-time favourites to those with professional facilities and large audience-space where established rock groups or jazz combos put on popular and well-advertised gigs. Many pubs have occasional music, or try it on a regular basis for a while and then give up because it's too expensive or there's not enough support. The ones in this section are all well-established – but live entertainment is always subject to change so do telephone before you make a journey, or check the weekly music press for full details.

In general, jazz is played in the bar itself
(non-enthusiasts betake themselves to another pub),
folk tends to be in a simple room out back or upstairs,
and rock in a separate music room with a stage and full
sound system. But there are always exceptions. Rock
pubs can get a little rough, though the better ones have
the right staff to evict potential trouble-makers in time.
Most of the pubs with a separate music room ask for
gate money, though it is rarely more than £2.00 and
often less.

Artesian
80 Chepstow Rd W2. 01-229 5912. *Charrington*. Big
Victorian boozer near the site of a long-lost artesian
well. There are pool tables in the public bar, a piano
player on Thur eves and varied live music on Sat
nights. Light snacks. **B.** *Music Thur & Sat eve.*

Battersea Show Palace   **4 R 8**
317 Battersea Park Rd SW11. 01-622 9060. *Courage*.
Lavish new entertainment pub, part cabaret and part
music hall, in which the bar staff are professional
singers and dancers who dish out the drinks before
launching into a full musical number on the stage
within the huge central bar. There is an entrance
charge. *Pub closed until 22.00. Entertainment every
night.*

Black Horse   **2 G 22**
6 Rathbone Pl W1. 01-580 0666. *Charrington*. The
Seven Dials jazz club arranges live music evenings
here. All types of jazz including some well-known
groups. **B.** *Music Tue & Sun.*

The Brewery Tap
47 Catherine Wheel Rd, Brentford. 01-560 5200.
Fullers. Dinky pub by a tributary of the Thames. On
Sun evening the resident pianist entertains. Food at
lunchtimes. **B.** *Music Sun eve.*

Bull and Gate
389 Kentish Town Rd NW5. 01-485 5358. *Charrington*.
Real ale and hot and cold snacks in the pub and at the

back, seven nights a week, live music – jazz, R & B or blues. **B.** *Music every eve.*

Bull's Head

373 Lonsdale Rd SW13. 01-876 5241. *Youngs.* Large Victorian building overlooking the Thames where top international jazz musicians play nightly and Sun lunchtimes. The only pub where Johnny Dankworth does a gig! Eat an excellent roast from the carvery at lunchtime or a good hot snack in the evening. The Stable Restaurant opens in the evenings for English food – steak, fish, home-made ice-cream, fruit pies cooked to order – and presents a traditional Sun lunch. For reservations phone 01-876 1855. Vegetarian food makes a nice addition. Can't be bettered for top quality jazz and home cooking. **B L D** *(Reserve* **D**). **£** or **££**. *Jazz every eve & Sun lunchtime.*

Chas and Dave's

109 Green Lanes N16. 01-226 5930. *Courage.* Large pub with a music lounge with excellent accoustics. The famous tenants appear only rarely, to drink Courage Best and entertain, but resident bands and visiting players produce a wide variety of styles. Tables alongside pub for fresh air drinking. **B.** *Music every eve.*

Cockney Pride   2 J 19

6 Jermyn St SW1. 01-930 5339. *Free House.* Nostalgic reconstruction of a Victorian Cockney pub, right down to the bubble and squeak! Fairly quiet at lunchtimes, and in the small bar in the evenings, but rumbustious in the big bar every night with piano sing-songs, contemporary rock, and country and western. **B L D**. **££**. *Music every eve.*

Empress of Russia   6 J 29

362 St John St EC1. 01-837 1910. *Whitbread.* Cheerful pub near Sadler's Wells Theatre. Saloon has hot and cold food at every session. Once upon a time there was a music hall in the room upstairs – now the Islington Folk Club meet there on a Thur and a ukulele band entertains every other Fri. Pay as you enter and take drinks in. **B.** *Music Thur & alt Fri eves.*

Greyhound
175 Fulham Palace Rd W6. 01-385 0526. *Watneys.*
Famous old pub with interior purpose-built for staging
music. Rock and pop from Mon to Sat with striptease
Sun–Fri lunchtime. **B.** *Entertainment Mon–Sat eve &
Sun–Fri lunchtime.*

Greyhound

Half Moon
93 Lower Richmond Rd, Putney SW15. 01-788 2387.
Youngs. Large pub with spacious back room where live
music is played nightly and on Sun lunchtime. Wide
range of music including jazz, R & B, rock, folk and
soul. Top names are billed here. **B.** *Music every eve &
Sun lunchtime.*

Half Moon Hotel
10 Half Moon Lane SE24. 01-274 2733. *Courage.*
Ritzy, chintzy pub with a big public-cum-saloon bar

and a licensed music room at the back which can hold up to 400 bodies. Local and visiting bands play a lively variety of rock, new wave, soul and R & B. Licence extends to *24.00 Thur–Sat.* **B.** *Music Thur–Sun eve.*

Hog's Grunt
The Production Village, 100 Cricklewood Lane NW2. 01-450 9361. *Charrington.* Part of the Production Village entertainment complex. Live music every night of the week. Mon is new bands night, Fri and Sat are for the well-established, Sun is jazz. *Music every eve. Licensed to 02.00.*

King's Head
4 Fulham High St SW6. 01-736 1413. *Charrington.* Large turn of the century building with a fairytale turret in the middle. Public bar has pool, darts and machine games. Lounge bar for music and dancing. Mainly rock and blues, but phone for details. Nice garden at the back, surrounded by trees. Priv rm. *Music every eve.*

King's Head 3 E 32
115 Upper St N1. 01-226 1916. *Ind Coope.* Famous theatre pub. Live music nightly after the stage performance. Folk, rock or jazz. **D** Mon–Sat eve before performance. *(Reserve).* **£.** *Music Mon–Sat.*

Minogues 3 D 32
80 Liverpool Rd N1. 01-359 4554. *Courage.* Beautifully decorated in belle epoch-style, this spacious pub is extremely popular. Irish meals are served in the lower seating area. Live music every night, generally traditional Irish, but also a smattering of other styles. **B.** *Music every eve.*

New Merlin's Cave 3 G 29
Margery St WC1. 01-837 2097. *Free House.* A barn-like place with a licensed music hall that can accommodate 250 people. Large lounge, with a buffet which serves hot or cold food continuously. Real ale. Live pop or rock every night. Famous for its Sun lunchtime jazz sessions. **B.** *Music every eve & Sun lunchtime.*

Pied Bull 1 B 3

1 Liverpool Rd N1. 01-837 3218. *Charrington*. Once Sir Walter Raleigh's house and reputedly one of the first buildings in England to encounter tobacco smoke.• Now a pleasant pub with a lounge bar complete with stage and dance floor. Every night of the week but Mon first-class performers belt out Fusion Jazz, R & B, blues or African jazz rhythm. *Licensed to 24.00 Mon–Thur, to 02.00 Fri & Sat.* **B.** *Music Tue–Sun eve.*

Pimlico Tram 5 O 16

6 Charlwood St SW1. 01-828 0448. *Charrington*. One long bar decorated with photographs of trams and maps of former tram routes. Resident organist plays pop music Fri & Sat evenings. **B.** *Music Fri & Sat eve.*

Plough

90 Stockwell Rd SW9. 01-274 3879. *Trumans*. In the public – darts and pool; in the saloon – good quality mainstream jazz, blues or rock. **B.** *Music Wed–Sun eve.*

Red Lion

318 High Rd, Brentford Middx. 01-560 6181. *Fullers*. Bands play seven nights a week – usually R & B and soul. Entry fee for the evenings but the Sun lunchtime sessions are free. Bar snacks anytime. **B.** *Music every eve & Sun lunchtime.*

Ruskin Arms

386 High St North, Manor Park E12. 01-472 0377. *Charrington*. Large pub with a boxing gymnasium upstairs and one or two well-known boxing faces in the bar. Not much food, just sandwiches. Separate music hall where visiting bands play heavy rock. **B.** *Music Thur–Mon eve.*

Sir George Robey

240 Seven Sisters Rd N4. 01-263 4581. *Taylor Walker*. Once associated with the old Finsbury Park Empire where Marie Lloyd, Harry Champion and George Robey played to packed audiences. Robey himself is said to have drunk here. There's a painting of him outside and the saloon is lined with photos of his act.

Irish-run now, with music every night and selected lunchtimes. Mostly Irish folk songs with some English and American thrown in. **B.** *Music every eve & some lunchtimes.*

The Swan   **4** K   2
1 Fulham Bdwy SW6. 01-385 1840. *Courage.* Real ale, traditional pub games and hot lunches on weekdays. A welcome new venue for R & B, blues and rock bands. **B.** *Music Mon–Sun eve.*

Tally Ho
Fortress Rd, Kentish Town NW5. 01-485 1210. *Watneys.* Victorian exterior and very 80s interior – although the beer and the jazz remain traditional. Hearty meals at every session. **B.** *Music most eves.*

Tankard   **5** Q 22
111 Kennington Rd SE11. 01-735 1517. *Charrington.* Opposite the Imperial War Museum. Comfortable and friendly. Sporty public bar with pool table, dart board and electronic games. Piano weekends, often inspiring a sing-song. **B.** *Music Thur–Sun eve & Sun lunchtime.*

Torrington
4 Lodge Lane N12. 01-445 4710. *Whitbread.* Well known on the pub circuit for some top names in jazz rock. Resident and visiting bands play in the restaurant, which is also available for party catering. Proper meals from the bar. Priv rm. **B.** *Music Fri & Sun eve.*

Tufnell Park Tavern
Tufnell Park Rd N7. 01-272 2078. *Courage.* The 1930s decor provides a suitable backdrop for the frequent jazz sessions. A popular pub serving real ale and hot and cold meals (not Sun). **B.** *Music Wed–Sun eve.*

The Water Rats   **3** G 27
328 Gray's Inn Rd WC1. 01-837 7269. *Courage.* 'The' place to go for old-time music hall. Decorated with music hall mirrors and posters. Always full of cheerful participating regulars. Hot food available on music hall nights. Booking essential. Ring the pub itself or Abadaba, the company who put on the excellent

shows, on 01-722 5395. No need to book for Sun to
Wed when you can enjoy the old-time dance band, or
light jazz or rock. *Thur–Sat open to 21.30. Live music
Sun–Wed; Music hall Thur–Sat.*

White Lion 3 I 31
37 Central St EC1. 01-253 4975. *Whitbread.* Typical
and traditional East End pub. Plenty of Victoriana and
an impressive old grand piano on which classic
sing-along songs are beaten out. **B.** *Music Fri–Mon.*

Yorkshire Grey 3 H 25
2 Theobald's Rd WC1. 01-405 2519. *Free House.*
Old-fashioned, wood-panelled saloon with jazz Thur
and Sun and two guitarists on Sat. The upstairs cocktail
bar is sometimes hired out for parties. Real ales are
brewed on the premises – City, Headline, Holborn,
and the extra-strong Regiment. **B.** *Music Thur, Sat &
Sun eve.*

REAL ALE SPECIALS ⎯⎯⎯

Real ale is, in a sense, alive. It continues to mature in
its cask in the pub cellar, and has to be pumped to the
bar by a beer engine. Keg beer, by contrast, is filtered
and pasturised before it leaves the brewery and is
brought to the bar by means of carbon dioxide pressure
which makes it unnaturally fizzy. Real ale only lasts for
a few days and must be well cared for or it will 'go off'.
Keg beer keeps for months and doesn't undergo any
change. All of this adds up to the fact that keg beer
gives the publican an easier life, which is why
traditional or 'real' ale began to vanish and the pubs
which served it became rarities.
Now, thanks to the determination and tireless
vigilance of the Campaign for Real Ale – CAMRA for
short – the majority of London's pubs serve at least one
real ale and a significant number can offer a choice.
This happy situation means that a section entitled Real
Ale Pubs would have to include virtually every pub in

this guide. However – there are real ale pubs which have an especial appeal to enthusiasts. These are the ones which serve several different ales, and change stock frequently, so that a regular visitor can work through a great many of Britain's varied brews without travelling the country.

Another welcome development is the spread of pubs which now brew beer on the premises; this tends to be greeted as an innovation but is in fact a reversion to the usual practice in the middle ages, when landlord and brewer tended to be the same person. In many of these home-brew pubs it is possible to watch part of the process. Two, three or four ales are generally produced, and be warned that there is almost always one extra-strong number which should be approached with caution by all but the most seasoned drinkers.

The Beer Shop

Pitfield St N1. 01-739 3701. Not a pub, an off-licence, but well worth knowing about, not only for its huge stock of British and bottled beers but also for its three home brews, produced by traditional methods in nearby Hoxton Square. Try Pitfield Bitter, or something a little stronger, Hoxton Heavy. If your taste runs to dark beer, Dark Star might rise to your expectations. *Open Mon–Fri 11.00–19.30; Sat 10.00–16.00.*

Bricklayer's Arms

63 Charlotte Rd EC2. 01-739 5245. *Free House.* Very jolly and a paradise for real ale enthusiasts – more than 50 are juggled around among seven hand pumps. At lunchtime it's a City pub, in the evening a traditional East End boozer. Hilarity often spills out on to the pavement in good weather. Small restaurant upstairs serves lunches. **B L. £.**

Bridge House

Tower Bridge Rd SE1. 01-403 2276. *Free House.* An ex-warehouse which became a pub and small brewery at the beginning of the 80s. They pull pints of their own Bermondsey Bitter for businessmen, and of '007' for those who like something with more impact. Pub grub at lunchtime, sandwiches in the evening. **B.**

FIRKIN PUBS

A seemingly ever-extending chain of welcoming pubs opened by David Bruce to revive the ancient craft of brewing on the premises. Firkin pubs are traditional in style, with wood floors and furniture, brass and glass, home-cooked food, heartily filled baps and, sometimes, a pianist to entertain. Their own beers are brewed beneath the feet of those who enjoy them, and part of the operation can usually be glimpsed through a strategically placed window or porthole. Most of the Firkin pubs also have guest ales on the pumps as a regular feature. (A firkin is half a kilderkin, or, if you prefer, a quarter-barrel sized cask).

Falcon and Firkin
360 Victoria Park Rd E9. 01-985 0693. *Bruce's Brewery*. Try Falcon Ale or, for something stronger, Bruce's Hackney Bitter. This pub features a family room and a pretty beer garden. **B.**

Ferret and Firkin in the Balloon up the Creek 4 M 5
114 Lots Rd, Chelsea SW10. 01-352 4645. *Bruce's Brewery*. Has taken over from 'I am the Only Running

Ferret & Firkin in the Balloon Up the Creek

Footman' as the pub with the longest name in London. Try Stoat or Ferret Ale. The aptly named Dogbolter is sometimes available, and there are draught ciders, country wines and a 'sing-a-long' pianist nightly. **B.**

Flounder and Firkin
54 Holloway Rd N7. 01-609 9574. *Bruce's Brewery.* Fish T'Ale or Whale Ale are the ones to get hooked on here – in a Firkin pub the puns are an essential part of the ambience. **B.**

Fox and Firkin
316 Lewisham High St SE13. 01-690 8925. *Bruce's Brewery.* Victorian wood, brass and glass interior, a nice garden and a piano player most evenings. Claims to be the first pub to bring smoked salmon to Lewisham. **B.**

Frog and Firkin
41 Tavistock Cres W11. 01-727 9250. *Bruce's Brewery.* Interesting collection of hats, a garden, a regular piano player and, to drink, Tavistock and Bullfrog. On special occasions there's Slaybelles, which refreshes parts you didn't even know you had. **B.**

Fuzzock and Firkin
77 Castle Rd NW1. 01-267 4855. *Bruce's Brewery.* If you're wondering what a fuzzock is – and not many dictionaries seem to know – the answer is in the beer, Ass Ale. **B.**

Goose and Firkin
47 Borough Rd SE1. 01-403 3590. *Bruce's Brewery.* The first of the Firkin pubs, friendly, wood-floored and brass decorated. Goose, Borough Bitter, Dogbolter, and sometimes the intensely powerful Gobstopper are on the pumps. **B.**

Phantom and Firkin
140 Balaam St E13. 01-472 2024. *Bruce's Brewery.* One of the most recent additions. Taste the ghostly Phantom Ale or the more haunting Spook Bitter. **B.**

Pheasant and Firkin   3 H 31
166 Goswell Rd EC1. 01-253 7429. *Bruce's Brewery.*

Handy for the Barbican Centre. Regulars tend to get stuck into backgammon and cribbage at weekend lunchtimes. Pheasant and Barbarian ales. **B.**

Phoenix and Firkin

Denmark Hill Railway Station, 5 Windsor Walk SE25. 01-701 8282. *Bruce's Brewery*. Largest and smartest of the Firkin pubs, the 'flagship' of the group, with all the familiar features of real ale – Rail Ale, actually, and Phoenix Bitter – and well-filled baps. **B.**

Hole in the Wall   6 N 23

5 Mepham St SE1. 01-928 6196. *Free House*. Built into the arches by Waterloo Station. One bar has a juke-box and pinball machine, the other is quieter though there is always the buzz of real ale lovers. Eight real ales always on the go – including Ruddle's, Godson's and Youngs. Mercy Stout from Cork is something special to try. **B.**

The Moon   3 H 25

18 New North St WC1. 01-405 6723. *Free House*. Victorian pub which began life as The George and Dragon and became notorious as a meeting place for thieves and footpads. Taken over by the proprietor of the Sun Inn, who changed the name and introduced a dozen real ales. Totally different in personality from its brother Sun – more of a comfortable family local. Priv rm. **B.**

Radnor Arms   1 G 4

247 Warwick Rd W14. 01-603 3224. *Free House*. It's only small, but the cellars are well-stocked – Royal Oak, Everard's Tiger, Adnam's and two guest beers which are changed every ten days or so. There is also draught cider. Full meals Mon to Fri lunchtimes (one dish for vegetarians, one for carnivores) and snacks on Sat. **B.**

Sun Inn   3 H 26

63 Lamb's Conduit St WC1. 01-405 8278. *Clifton Inns*. Small, tatty, bustling and rumbustious, with immense, old vaulted cellars spreading under the streets which make it possible to store up to 70 real ales and to make

20 available at any one time, including little known but excellent guest beers. Home delivery by the barrel can be arranged. **B.**

Three Kings   **1** F   2
171 North End Rd W14. 01-603 6071. *Free House*. This was once the Nashville Rooms, known for its visiting bands and hard-wearing dance floor. It has now been turned into an enormous ('like the Queen Mary') temple of real ale with 29 handpumps dispensing a minimum of 9 real ales, four lagers and three keg beers, not to mention a draught cider. Regulars are Wadworth 6X, Marston's Pedigree, Samuel Smith's Old Brewery Bitter, Fullers London Pride, Ruddles and Abbott Ale. Hot food at every session and traditional Sun lunches. **B.**

Truscott Arms
55 Shirland Rd W9. 01-286 0310. *Free House*. The promise implied in the row of 10 handpumps is not an idle one – there are 10 different real ales on the go at any one time. (The Truscott Ten refers not to these but to the fact that anyone who downs 10 pints in one session gets his or her name in gold on a special board – whether or not he or she can focus on it). Hot and cold lunches Mon to Fri and pizzas and toasties in the evening. Priv rm. **B.**

Victoria   **3** A 24
2 Mornington Ter NW1. 01-387 3804. *Whitbread*. Eight real ales here, including Devenish Wessex Bitter, Badger, Samuel Smith's, Fullers, Greene King, Adnam's and Whitbreads' Castle Eden Ale, in a pleasant family atmosphere. In the unlikely event you grow weary of drinking, there's hot and cold food from Mon to Sat and barbecues in the garden during summer weekends. **B.**

Welch Bros
130 High Rd, East Finchley N2. 01-444 7444. *Free House*. The 12 hand pumps pull about 100 different real ales in a year. Those which are pretty well always on are Ruddles, Charles Wells' Bombardier, Courage Director's, Boddington's, Archers Headbanger and

Willie Warmer. (Tread cautiously with the last two). There are also six lagers, 17 country wines and food at every session (light on a Sun). **B**.

OUTDOOR DRINKING ———

Pubs which have facilities for open-air drinking in good weather – in a garden or on a terrace or patio – are especially popular with families, who are glad to be able to take the children along and drink outside with them. They are also popular with anyone who needs a breather during a stuffy London summer. Many places offer specifically outdoor diversions, like barbecues or the opportunity to stare at passers-by from a comfortable seat. Here are some good summertime pubs. They open during the usual pub hours, unless otherwise stated. There are still more pubs with outdoor drinking facilities along the banks of the Thames and in the outskirts of London and beyond. See also the sections on **Riverside** and **Richmond & Kew**.

Admiral Codrington   4 J 11
17 Mossop St SW3. 01-589 4603. *Charrington*. Large and alluring range of malt whiskies in this wood-panelled, gas-lit house with its nice antique mirrors. The modern horoscope pictures in the grill-and-carvery aren't too much of a shock. Big garden with overhanging grape vine, and barbecues in good weather. Good 'up-market' Chelsea local, complete with cocktail bar. **B L D**. *Closed D Sat & Sun*. **££**.

Antwerp Arms
168 Church Rd N17. 01-808 4449. *Charrington*. In a rural corner of a suburban area, next to All Hallows Church, and given its name in the 19th century when the brewery won an award in Antwerp. Pretty paved garden, with shrubs and roses in the beds around the edge, a fishpond and a cherry tree. Decorative ceiling in the one bar. **B**.

Bunch of Grapes   6 Q 29
2 St Thomas's St SE1. 01-407 3673. *Free House*. Has
become a pub again (after a brief experience as a wine
bar called The Loose Vine). Hot snacks in the bar,
grills in the upstairs restaurant, Young's and
Brakespears ale to drink. Pleasant garden at the back –
families welcome. **B L** *(Reserve)*. *Closed Sat & Sun*. **££.**

Canonbury Tavern
21 Canonbury Pl N1. 01-226 1881. *Charrington*.
Popular local. A good place to take the kids as there is
a large garden at the back with tables, chairs and even
children's rides. Imaginative well-prepared food at the
bar – including hot dogs to take outside. There's been a
tavern on the site since the 16th century, though this
building is a mere 200 years old. **B L. £.**

Cross Keys   4 M 8
2 Lawrence St SW3. 01-352 1893. *Courage*. Popular
Chelsea local with exceptionally friendly staff and an
extensive cold table. Outside, a pretty walled garden,
with plants scattered around. They never pull up the
weeds because they look nice where they are! **B.**

Duke of Clarence   1 A 5
203 Holland Park Av W11. 01-603 5431. *Charrington*.
400-year-old pub that was rebuilt in 1939 with a
medieval style interior and a Victorian bar. Beautiful
flagged courtyard with imitation gas lamps and its own
conservatory bar. Good selection of food, regular
barbecues in the summer and occasional evenings of
live jazz or classical music. **B.** *Pub opens 19.00 Sat eve.*

Duke of Somerset   6 P 33
Little Somerset St, Aldgate E1. 01-481 0785.
Charrington. Boasts of being the only City pub with a
patio garden – certainly it has a nice one, as well as a
large and usually crowded bar, a real ale or two, and
bar snacks at every session. One of the few in the area
that doesn't close at weekends. **B.**

Earl of Lonsdale
277/281 Westbourne Grove W11. 01-727 6335. *Samuel
Smith*. Behind the antique stalls of the Portobello
Road market stands this large, comfortable mid-

Victorian pub, serving Old Brewery Bitter and bar lunches. Outside, very much a town garden, with stone flags and street lamps, softened by the welcome presence of a lovely Iolanthus tree. **B.**

Flask

77 Highgate West Hill N6. 01-340 3969. *Taylor Walker*. Old world tavern named for the flasks which people used to buy here to fill with water at the Hampstead wells. Dick Turpin once hid in the cellars and Hogarth drew in the bar (though not simultaneously). On fine days, everyone crowds on to the large forecourt, with its rustic tables and benches. Sometimes there are Morris dancers to watch – if not, there are always the comings and goings of the rich and famous who live in The Grove, opposite, not to mention Burton's and Tetley's Bitter to drink. **B L** *Mon–Fri (Reserve)*. **£.**

Freemason's Arms

32 Downshire Hill NW3. 01-435 4498. *Charrington*. Popular Hampstead pub, often full of familiar television faces. Boasts of having the largest pub garden in London, with an upper and lower terrace, a small summerhouse; rustic furniture and lots of roses. Also a court for pell mell – a kind of old English skittles or lawn billiards – and an indoor skittle alley. **B.**

Hare and Hounds

216 Upper Richmond Rd West SW14. 01-876 4304. *Youngs*. First a courthouse, then a coaching inn, now a pleasant middle-aged pub with lots of copper pans, hunting horns and friendly gas fires. The snooker table is in the saloon bar. The large garden can be reached by a separate entrance. **B.**

Hand in Hand

6 Crooked Billet SW19. *Youngs*. A beautiful old pub on the edge of Wimbledon Common where you can take your drink in summer. Very popular with a good selection of beers and a restaurant at the back. **B L D. ££.**

Jack Straw's Castle

North End Way NW3. 01-435 8885. *Charrington*. Rebuilt in the 60s on the site of the original pub.

Named for Wat Tyler's closest comrade who was hanged just outside. Unusual weatherboard frontage, and marvellous views over the Heath. Courtyard with tables and chairs for sunny days. There is a snack bar, a cocktail bar, and the Castle Carving Room for traditional roasts. Priv rm. **B L D** *(Reserve)*. *Closed* **L** *Sat*. **££.**

Ladbroke Arms   1 A   6
54 Ladbroke Rd W11. 01-727 6648. *Clifton Inns.* Charming 18th-century pub won by Lord Ladbroke in a gambling debt. Arresting floral arrangements and wooden bench seating in the pretty forecourt, which has recently won prizes from both brewery and council. Highly thought of home-cooked food and salads. No food Sun eve. **B.**

Mudlark   6 Q 30
Off Tooley St, London Bridge SE1. 01-403 1517. *Charrington.* The Mudlarks of Dickensian London were pathetic waifs who scavenged for coins and other treasures at the river's edge. Their modern counterparts tend to be well-fed and equipped with metal detectors. The pub which bears their name has two smart floors, a patio garden overlooking the 'piazza' of a new local development, and extensive bar snacks. **B.** *Pub closed Sat eve & Sun.*

Phene Arms   4 M   9
9 Phene St SW3. 01-352 8391. *Watneys.* Named after Dr Phene, the first man to plant trees in cities. Appropriately enough, this small cul-de-sac pub is almost hidden by trees. In fine weather, sit drinking on the patio with trees for company and flowers for colour. Inside, the high ceiling and long windows give a pleasant illusion of space. The upstairs restaurant serves lunch and dinner from Mon to Sat. Priv rm. **B. L D** *Mon to Sat.* **£** or **££.**

Railway Bell
14 Cawnpore St SE19. 01-670 2844. *Youngs.* Attractive, well-cared-for walled garden with two rows of umbrella-shaded tables. Lots of railway pictures line the walls of the long bar. The base for the local Morris

Men. Won the 1981 Standard Pub of the Year contest. Super hot lunches. **B.**

The Raj   1 A 5
40 Holland Park Av W11. 01-727 6322. *Watneys.* Victorian pub recently redecorated in carefully researched reproduction British Raj style. At the back is a paved garden with a gazebo, and in front there are benches and tables. Snacks are served downstairs at lunchtime and the new restaurant upstairs is open in the evenings from Mon to Sat for bar snacks or full meals – wide range of food including,of course, a Raj Curry. **B D** *(Mon–Sat).* **£.**

Scarsdale Arms   1 E 5
23a Edwardes Sq W8. 01-937 1811. *Semi-Free House.* In winter, sit amidst old clocks and plates, gas lamps, stuffed animals and frosted glass windows in front of an open fire. In summer, sit out under the plane trees on the pretty terrace. Very good bar lunches and real ales. There is a carol singing night late in December. **B.**

Sir Christopher Hatton   3 I 28
Leather Lane EC1. 01-405 4226. *Charrington.* Mock Tudor design, out of respect to Sir Christopher who lived when Tudor design was the latest thing. Stone floors, wooden beams, pew seating and a large patio, with flowering tubs and low chaining, in the pedestrian precinct where a street market flourishes until early afternoon. There's a cold buffet all day and hot snacks at lunchtime. **B.** *Pub closed Sat eve & all Sun.*

Spaniard's Inn
Spaniard's Rd NW3. 01-455 3276. *Charrington.* Once the residence of the Spanish Ambassador to the Court of James I, then a pub run by two Spanish brothers who took it over in about 1620. Shelley, Keats, Byron and Joshua Reynolds drank here – so, inevitably, did Dickens, who set a scene of 'The Pickwick Papers' in the garden. This is large and very pretty with roses, paving, a lawn and its own bar. An upstairs bar called Turpin's Room opens in the eve. Dick Turpin was very active around here and is said still to ride past on certain nights. Bar meals available both sessions. **B.**

Swan Tavern   **1 B 10**
55 Bayswater Rd W2. 01-262 5204. *Watneys*. This
popular beer garden, opposite the park and handy for
central London, is illuminated from dusk on. It has
become a rendezvous for overseas visitors. Juke-box
plays continuously and a uniformed chef carves cold
joints at both sessions. **B.**

The Victoria
10 West Temple Sheen, East Sheen SW14. 01-876
4238. *Watneys*. Lovely big garden, which has won two
or three awards, with a large conservatory for dodgy
weather. Barbecued food is served in the conservatory
Mon to Sat evenings. Full menu at lunchtime, Mon to
Sat, and they'll serve it to you outside if you wish.
Friendly, comfortable, country-type pub, popular with
all ages. **B.**

Windmill Inn, Ye Olde
Clapham Common South Side SW4. 01-673 4578.
Youngs. Popular and lively with two separate patios,
one decorated with plants in tubs, the other a forest of
swings, slides and roundabouts. The Grill room
operates on weekday lunchtimes and you can get
snacks on a Sat. **B L.** *Closed* **L** *Sun*. **££.**

Windsor Castle   **1 C 7**
114 Campden Hill Rd W8. 01-727 8491. *Charrington*.
Built in 1835 when it was actually possible to see
Windsor Castle from here. There are three bars, with
low beamed ceilings and open fires. The large walled
garden has a bar and snack bar of its own (to which it
doesn't admit children), and plants in hanging baskets.
Full meals all the time except Sun eve. **B L D. £.**

RIVERSIDE PUBS ⎯⎯⎯⎯⎯⎯

The Thames is an immensely varied river and a pub
crawl along its London banks ranges from leafy limpid
calm to haunted Dickensian wharves. The river enters
London from a green and pleasant part of Surrey (see
the section on **Richmond & Kew**), passes through

Chiswick with its moored barges and Georgian waterfront houses, and then flows on from Mortlake to Putney, on which stretch the two oldest universities hold their annual battle for rowing supremacy. At Wandsworth and Battersea it becomes industrial on its south bank while on its north, at Chelsea, it is literary and artistic. At Westminster it passes the Houses of Parliament and the Abbey on one side, and the South Bank Complex on the other. Through the City and the Pool of London, it becomes glamorously creepy with its history of thieves and smugglers, and fugitives from the Tower. At Greenwich it slides past the famous Observatory and Wren's imposing Naval College and continues out of London by way of the new Thames Flood Barrier and ancient docks.

All along its banks there are pubs, some of them extremely old. Many have balconies or terraces where you may sit overlooking the water. Others open straight on to the towpath and don't mind if you carry your drinks to the edge, though they do wish you'd bring your glasses back. Quite a number can be reached by walking along the towpath (the towpath walk is being opened up in stages and is now nearly complete), and some others can be reached by way of the passenger ferry which ploughs up and down river from Richmond to Greenwich. Failing either of these appropriate approaches, there are always buses or tubes.

Anchor   6 O 28
Bankside SE1. 01-407 1577. *Courage*. The original pub on this site, whose clientele was a hideous mixture of smugglers, press gangs and warders from The Clink, was destroyed in the fire of 1666. The present building is 18th century with exposed beams, open fires, rough walls, five small bars and three restaurants, one with a minstrels' gallery as well as an upstairs barbecue bar. Plenty of antique bric-a-brac and a first edition of Dr Johnson's Dictionary. Restaurant serves hearty English meals. Try the Anchor Special of rib of beef, and Mrs Thrale's Snack Bar offers hot food at every session. **B L D** *(Reserve)*. **££.**

Angel
101 Bermondsay Wall East SE16. 01-237 3608.
Courage. 15th-century Thameside pub on piles, with a
pillared balcony overlooking the river and the Pool of
London. Riverish decor with wrought iron lamps, a
ship's steering wheel and prints of the area as it once
was. Samuel Pepys drank here and so did Captain
Cook. English cuisine in the restaurant with a fishy bias
– smoked fish starters, Scotch grills, Greenwich fish
pie, some game. **B L D.** *Closed* **L** *Sat,* **D** *Sun.* **£££.**

Barmy Arms
Riverside, Twickenham, Middx. 01-892 0863.
Watneys. Another pub with a boating theme in its two
bars. Very old – built as a school in about 1400 and
converted to its present purpose in 1729, since when
nothing structural has been changed. Good snacks,
roast lunches, and a patio where you can drink and
contemplate Eel Pie Island. **B.**

Bell
8 Thames St, Hampton, Middx. 01-979 1444. *Taylor
Walker*. Small, cosy pub next to the church with river
views, real ales, lunchtime snacks and full Sun lunches.
B.

Bell and Crown
13 Thames Rd, Chiswick W4. 01-994 4164. *Fullers*.
Born-again Victoriana, on an old pub site as the prints
on the wall testify. Has recently added a Victorian
verandah with lovely river views. Real ale on
hand-pumps and bar meals at lunchtime, sandwiches
anytime. **B.**

Bishop Out Of Residence
Bishop's Hall, Thames St, Kingston. 01-546 4965.
Youngs. New pub on the site of the home of a bishop
said to have 'gone fishing' more often than he ought.
Meals (not Sun evenings), snacks, real ale and a
riverside terrace. **B.**

Black Lion
2 South Black Lion Lane W6. 01-748 7056. *Watneys*.
Lovely 400-year-old riverside pub. Prize-winning

paved garden with shrubs, flowerbeds and window boxes. Featured as The Black Swan in A.P. Herbert's 'The Water Gypsies'. Quiet games in the single bar – cribbage, backgammon and chess. Beers both traditional and Australian and good food at all times. **B.**

Blue Anchor
13 Lower Mall, Hammersmith W6. 01-748 5774. *Courage*. Started life as The Blew Anchor and Washhouses, and was first licensed under its present name in 1720. One wood-panelled bar attracting those in search of Director's and Best Bitter. Very crowded, usually with a younger crowd in the evenings, including people from the two rowing clubs next door. In summer, take your pint and lean on the river wall to watch the water flowing by. **B.**

Bull's Head
Strand on the Green, Chiswick W4. 01-994 0647. *Richmond Taverns*. 350-year-old Chiswick waterfront tavern with exposed blackened beams. Old world atmosphere not dispersed by the video machines, darts and bar billiards. Has pictures of its own history on the wall, including the original plans. There is also a framed page of manuscript explaining how Cromwell was nearly caught here by the pursuing Royalists. Well-stocked salad and buffet bar. **B.**

City Barge
27 Strand on the Green, Chiswick W4. 01-994 2148. *Courage*. Along from the Bull's Head is this 15th century Elizabethan charter inn. Originally called The Navigator's Arms. Given its present name in the late 19th century because the Lord Mayor's barge used to be moored nearby. Low ceiling'd old bar is festooned with aged china. Downstairs bar becomes an à la carte restaurant Mon to Fri lunchtime. Wander on to the towpath with your drink to watch passing boats or bobbing ducks. **B L** *(Mon–Fri)*. **££.**

Cutty Sark
Ballast Quay, Lassell St SE10. 01-858 3146. *Free House*. Quiet Georgian pub, enhanced by bay

windows and wooden interior, overlooks the river and wharves. Stands downstream from its namesake which is in dry dock. Sometimes, in summertime, Morris men dance outside. Restaurant, on three levels, offers traditional English food with some suitably fishy additions. Whitebait suppers in the bar. **B L D.** *Closed* **D** *Sun, L Sat & Mon.* **££.**

Dickens Inn   6 R 32
St Katharine's Way E1. 01-488 1226. *Free House*. Fine views of the yacht marina and Tower Bridge from this artfully converted historic warehouse. Exposed beams, antique furniture, a brass-topped bar and sawdust on the floor. Real ale, including Dickens' own, and food on three levels. Pub grub in the Tavern Room on the ground floor; English food à la carte in the Pickwick Room on the first floor (01-488 2208 for bookings); various fish dishes in the Dickens Room on the top floor (01-488 9932 for bookings). **B L D** *(Reserve).* **£££.**

Dove
19 Upper Mall W6. 01-748 5405. *Fuller, Smith and Turner*. Mellow 1700s pub with a terrace overlooking the river. Dark oak beams, soft lights, very traditional – James Thomson wrote 'Rule Britannia' here and you can't get much more British than that. Hot and cold buffet at lunchtime. **B.**

Duke's Head
8 Lower Richmond Rd, Putney SW15. 01-788 2552. *Youngs*. Lots of nice Victorian engraved glass in this cream painted house near the start of the Oxford and Cambridge Boat Race. Full lunches served in the airy lounge bar, with its large windows overlooking a very rowing-orientated part of the river. In fact, a local rowing club stores its boats underneath. **B.**

Founders Arms   6 N 27
Bankside SE1. 01-928 1899. *Youngs*. One of London's newest pubs, built on the site of the foundry where the bells of St Paul's were cast. There is a good view across the river to St Paul's itself. Single, J-shaped bar with smart mahogany and velvet decor and an eminently

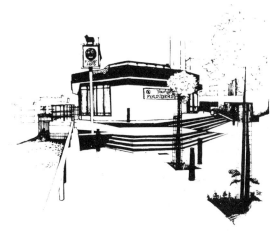

Founders Arms

respectable clientele. Food from the salad bar or the table d'hôte and à la carte restaurant. Beer from the famous brewery up the river. **B L D** *(Reserve)*. *Closed* **L** *Sat,* **D** *Sun.* **££.**

Gazebo
King's Passage, Kingston. 01-546 4495. *Samuel Smith*. Good bar lunches and Old Brewery Bitter from the wood in this large house with its two Edwardian gazebos. The balconied first floor offers comfortable seating and the best river views. Seats at the water's edge, too. **B.**

Grapes
76 Narrow St E14. 01-987 4396. *Taylor Walker*. London's old Docklands are being lavishly developed and the pub is well within the area where warehouses are being transmogrified into apartment blocks. Good view up and down river from the verandah. Real ale, bar snacks and a dining room specializing in fish – fish soups, oysters in season, Dover sole, several puddings. Reputed to be the pub called The Six Jolly Fellowship Porters in Dickens' 'Our Mutual Friend'. **B L D** *(Reserve).* **££.**

Gun
27 Coldharbour Lane E14. 01-987 1692. *Ind Coope*.
Near the West India dock and said to have been the
setting for a meeting between Lord Nelson and Lady
Hamilton. There is a public bar and two riverside bars,
with good views of an industrial part of the Thames. **B**.

London Apprentice
62 Church St, Old Isleworth, Middx. 01-560 6136.
Watneys. Very famous 15th-century Thameside pub,
with lovely Elizabethan and Georgian interiors,
decorated with prints of Hogarth's 'Apprentices'. Got
its name in the days when the apprentices from
London's Docks spent their one day-off a year rowing
down here for a pint or two. Large flowery patio with a
conservatory restaurant right on the river and a
first-floor restaurant overlooking it. Restaurant
(01-560 1915) serves traditional English food – with
ribs of beef their speciality. **B L D** *(Reserve)*. **££**.

Mayflower
117 Rotherhithe St SE16. 01-237 4088. *Charrington*.
Tudor Inn which was christened The Shippe but
changed its name when the Mayflower, which set off
from this part of the river, reached America. Stand
drinking on the jetty and ponder on the Pilgrim
Fathers. The only pub in England licensed to sell
English and American postage stamps. You can always
get a hot snack or salad – for the international
restaurant it's wise to book. **B L** *Mon–Fri*. **D** *Mon–Sat*
(Reserve). **££**.

Mitre Hotel
Hampton Court Bridge, Surrey. 01-979 2264.
Trumans. Big and popular with a large garden which is
open all day in summer. Eat and drink at a table by the
river or have a full meal in the Steak House
Restaurant. Receptions and banquets are regularly
catered for. **B L D. £** or **££**.

Old Justice
94 Bermondsey Wall East SE16. 01-237 3452.
Charrington. A well-hidden riverside pub with fine
views looking on to Tower Bridge. Timber-panelled

with dropped beams, this is a London local which could just as well be at home in the heart of Surrey. **B.**

Old Ship
25 Upper Mall W6. 01-748 2593. *Watneys.* Mid 17th century pub (the oldest in Hammersmith) warmly refurbished, with a terrace overlooking the Thames. In winter, the open fire is the first thing you see as you walk in. For your entertainment, a juke-box, pool and video machines. Good snack bar, open day and evening. Children welcome. Priv rm. **B.**

Pope's Grotto
Cross Deep, Twickenham, Middx. 01-892 3050. *Youngs.* Large, post-war pub with rear patio for summer barbecues. Carvery and cold food at every session except Sun eve. Good range of whiskies. Comfortable, modern if undistinguished interior, although the river view compensates. **B.**

Prospect of Whitby
57 Wapping Wall E1. 01-481 1095. *Watneys.* Historic dockland tavern dating back to the reign of Henry VIII. Samuel Pepys and Rex Whistler drank here, but then so did 'hanging' Judge Jeffries, not to mention such numbers of thieves and smugglers that it came to be called 'The Devil's Tavern'. Decorated with nautical souvenirs and fine pewter. Restaurant terrace overlooks the Thames. Inventive French cuisine with house specialities in season. Live music every eve in ground floor bar – type varies but it's usually lively. **B L D** *(Reserve). Closed* **L** *Sat.* **£££+.**

Rivers   5 O 21
35 Albert Embankment SW1. 01-735 3723. *Whitbread.* Late Victorian pub, more or less across the river from the Tate Gallery. Particularly good view from the restaurant upstairs where you can eat à la carte or from a set menu. Priv rm. **B L** *(Mon–Fri)* **D** *(Mon–Sat).* **£** or **££.**

Rose of York
Petersham Rd, Richmond. 01-940 0626. *Samuel Smith.* Used to be the Tudor Close, but its Yorkshire brewery

The Prospect of Whitby

gave it a new name to go with the refurbishing. Large,
comfortable, L-shaped bar panelled in English oak and
decorated with reproductions of paintings by Turner
and Reynolds of the famous 'turn in the river'. Terrace
and courtyard have good views across the water. Beer
from the wood and a home-cooked buffet. Carvery
open on Sun. **B.**

Rutland

Lower Mall, Hammersmith W6. 01-748 5586.
Watneys. Good place to extend your knowledge of
ale – guest beers come canned or bottled from all over
the world – France, Australia, Japan. Hot snacks
to accompany them if required. Mon is Curry Night,

Thur is Jazz Night and there's a roast lunch on a Sun. Priv rm. **B. L** *Sun.*

Samuel Pepys   **6** N 28
Brooks Wharf, 48 Upper Thames St EC4. 01-248 3048. *Charrington*. Warehouse converted into rambling pub with a two-tiered river-view terrace bar and a spacious cellar bar with well-stocked food counter. The light, airy restaurant has good views of the river. Solid English meals – game pie and spotted dick, perhaps. Transcriptions of Pepys' diaries and an original letter on display among the old lamps, prints and noticeboards. **B L D** *(Reserve). Closed* **L** *Sat.* **£££.**

Ship
Ship Lane SW14. 01-876 1439. *Watneys*. 16th century terraced pub in Mortlake, at the end of the line for the Oxford and Cambridge Boat Race. Usually has an extension on Boat Race Day. Traditional bar with a nautical theme – ship's wheel, ropes and suitable prints. Well-equipped children's playground in the garden. Priv rm. **B L. £.**

Sir Christopher Wren's House Hotel
Windsor, Berks. Windsor 61354. *Free House*. C. Wren really did live here; now an elegant hotel with an attractively vegetated paved courtyard overlooking the water near Eton Bridge. Coffees, teas and drinks are served to non-residents and the restaurant has French-cum-English food. **B L D.** *Closed* **L** *Sat.* **£££.**

Star and Garter
4 Lower Richmond Rd, Putney SW15. 01-788 0345. *Courage*. Huge riverside building which is a landmark from both sides of Putney Bridge. Hearty and friendly with very good lunches, Sun included. Beware of equinoxial parking by the river – spring and neap tides can bring the water lapping up to the pub's foundations. **B.**

Three Pigeons
87 Petersham Rd, Richmond. 01-940 0361. *Watneys*. Old riverside inn with a beer garden. Pigeons on the sign are outnumbered by those patrolling outside.

Restaurant sticks out over the water with windows all around so that virtually every table has a good view. English food. **B L D** *(Reserve)*. **££.**

Town of Ramsgate
62 Wapping High St E1. 01-488 2685. *Charrington.* 15th-century tavern with glamorously grisly past. The riverside garden, where children now play, was once the hanging dock for petty criminals. Secret tunnels are said to lead to the Tower of London. Wapping Old Stairs, alongside, was the scene of the capture of Captain Blood, who was making off with the Crown Jewels at the time, and the tavern itself saw the capture of the infamous Judge Jeffries. **B.**

Trafalgar Tavern
Park Row SE10. 01-858 2437. *Watneys.* On Thames-side at Greenwich, near Wren's imposing Naval College. All the bars have large windows overlooking the river. Upstairs bar looks like the inside of a ship. Pictures of Nelson and some early navigational instruments are on display. Relevant menu in restaurant – perhaps a plate of whitebait for starters then Sole Nelson or Turkey Breast Hamilton, and finally a wide choice of puddings. Priv rm. **L D** *(Reserve)*. *Closed* **D** *Sun,* **L D** *Mon.* **££.**

Waterman's Arms
1 Glenaffric Av E14. 01-538 0712. *Taylor Walker.* This one stands next door to a rowing club and has been newly decked out along maritime lines with oars and barrels in evidence and pictures of ships on the walls. Bar snacks available. **B.**

Waterman's Arms
12 Water Lane, Richmond. 01-940 2893. *Youngs.* One of the oldest pubs in Richmond and once a watering-hole for the watermen who trudged up Water Lane from the river. No water in the beer, however. Friendly, with a lot of regulars in its two linked bars. Active jukebox. **B.**

White Cross
Cholmondeley Walk, Richmond. 01-940 0909.

Youngs. Traditional Victorian pub with two open fireplaces, one rather curiously placed under a window. The garden runs down to the quayside. Bar food at every session and a carvery for heartier meals. **B L D.** *Closed* **D** *Sun.* **££.**

White Swan

Riverside, Twickenham. 01-892 2166. *Watneys*. Startlingly attractive black-and-white balconied pub, bright with geraniums and lobelia in summer. Plain and comfy inside, it stands right on the river's edge. Draught Guinness, Combes and Websters as well as Watney ales, and occasional live music. The excellent lunchtime food, Mon–Sat, is on from *13.00* (it comes in fresh daily and they need time to prepare it). **B.**

Yacht

5 Crane St SE10. 01-858 0175. *Watneys*. Originally 17th century but rebuilt after Second World War bombing. The one bar is decorated with photographs of some of the yachts which have competed for the Americas Cup. Outside terrace for good weather, and a large conservatory restaurant where children are welcome. Continental beers are often on offer, as well as British favourites, and they like to feed you, too; a full range of food from bar snacks to an à la carte restaurant menu is available at all times. At high tide the river laps against the windows. **B L D. £** or **££.**

EARLY OPENING PUBS ⎯⎯

Even in these days of more relaxed licensing laws there are not many pubs which choose to open for business at *06.00* in the morning. The exceptions are, and always have been, the few which are virtually on the doorstep of one of the major wholesale markets. Market trading usually starts as early as *04.00* or *05.00* and by *06.00* or *07.00* there are a great many people around feeling as though it's lunchtime and craving a drink, a meal, or both. Special licences mean that these cravings can be fulfilled and although, strictly, alcohol should only be served to bona fide market workers, it may not be easy for a licensee to discriminate since people wash and change before heading for refreshment and tend not to wander into a pub covered in blood or vegetables.

The only important market with no early-opening local is Billingsgate fish market, in its new site on the Isle of Dogs; Smithfield wholesale meat market is probably the best served, but New Covent Garden, Spitalfields, Borough Market and Stratford Market don't lose out.

Barley Mow   5 R 15
East Bridge, New Covent Garden Market SW8. 01-720 5555. *Courage.* Go right into the market itself for this one (there's a charge for cars) which serves full breakfasts, full lunches, and snacks throughout its opening hours. The customers are shiftworkers and traders from New Covent Garden fruit, vegetable and flower market, which moved here in 1974. Note short hours. **B.** *Open 05.00–15.00 Mon–Sat. Closed Sun.* **£.**

Fox and Anchor   6 J 28
115 Charterhouse St EC1. 01-253 4838. *Taylor Walker.* Behind a moulded stone art nouveau façade is a friendly old bar with separate restaurant section serving very full breakfasts and grilled lunches to the buyers and butchers of nearby Smithfield. It's wise to book for the set breakfast. Note limited opening hours. **B L.** *Open 06.00–15.00 Mon–Fri only. Closed Sat & Sun.* **£.**

Globe   6 P 28
8 Bedale St SE1. 01-407 0043. *Free House.* Handy for the fruit and veg dealers of Borough Market who can enjoy coffee, liqueurs, Draught Bass or a guest real ale in the early hours. There are plans to introduce food at the morning session – at the moment it's bar lunches only. **B.** *Open 06.30–08.30; 11.00–15.00 & 17.30–22.00 Tue–Fri; 06.30–08.30 & 11.00–15.00 Sat. Closed Sun & Mon.* **£.**

Gun   6 N 33
54 Brushfield St E1. 01-247 7988. *Trumans.* Friendly local to the Spitalfields fruit, flower and vegetable

market. Try coffee with a dash of brandy and maybe a round of toast – those in need of a full breakfast cross the road to Dino's. Upstairs restaurant serves steak-pie-and-chip-style lunches and customers can enjoy darts, pool and a real fire. **B L.** *Open 06.00–09.00; 11.00–15.00; 17.30–22.30 Mon–Fri; 06.00–09.00 Sat. Closed Sun.* **£.**

The Hope   6 J 29
94 Cowcross St EC1. 01-250 1442. *Watneys.* Why did the cow cross the street? To get to Smithfield Market in the days when it dealt in live animals as opposed to the other kind. Pretty 19th-century pub, with nice windows and mirrors, serving great breakfasts in the upstairs restaurant and also traditional English lunches. Hot meat-filled sandwiches are available over the bar. Portions are hearty – this is Smithfield after all. **B L.** *Open 06.00–09.00; 10.30–15.00 & 17.30–20.00 Mon–Fri. Closed Sat & Sun.* **£.**

Market Tavern   5 R 15
Market Towers, 1 Nine Elms Lane SW8. 01-622 5655. *Free House.* A pub with two distinct personalities. From five until nine it welcomes the workers from New Covent Garden Market. When it closes at nine it doesn't re-open until nine in the evening by which time it has transmogrified itself into a gay pub with a late licence which takes it through till the small hours. No food. *Open 05.00–09.00 Mon–Fri; 21.00 till late Mon–Sun.*

Newmarket   6 K 28
26 Smithfield St EC1. 01-248 3191. *Charrington.* The decor has a horsey flavour, the clientele in the two large bars tend to come from nearby Smithfield, and the atmosphere is bustling and crowded. No food at breakfast time but cooked lunches served on weekdays. **B.** *Open 06.30–09.30; 11.00–15.00; 17.30–23.00 Mon–Fri. Closed Sat & Sun.* **£.**

Railway Tavern
131 Angel Lane E15. 01-534 3123. *Charrington.* Amiable old Victorian pub with a comfortable bar and a games room for pool and darts. The early session is

for the benefit of the Stratford wholesale fruit and vegetable market. There are sandwiches in the morning, full bar meals at lunchtime and evening snacks. Beer garden, patio and real ale, too. No food on Sun. **B.** *Open 05.00–08.00; 11.00–15.00; 17.30–20.30 Mon–Sat; 12.00–14.00 & 19.00–22.00 Sun.* **£.**

Victoria   **6** J 28
25 Charterhouse St EC1. 01-405 1660. *Taylor Walker.* Recent refurbishment has turned this market pub into a bit of an up-market pub. There are full breakfasts, coffees and drinks to restore the workers at nearby Smithfield, also full lunches in the upstairs restaurant, and bar snacks at lunchtime and in the evening. **B L.** *Open 05.00–08.00; 11.00–15.00 & 17.30–20.30 Mon–Fri. Closed Sat & Sun.* **£.**

THEATRE PUBS

Some of the most exciting and varied fringe theatre takes place in rooms above or behind pubs – new plays, classics, cabaret, revues, musicals and monologues. The atmosphere is friendly and relaxed, with people wandering in from the bar carrying their drinks; sometimes it is possible to get a snack, or even a full meal, before the performance. It is wise to book in advance, but if you decide to go on the spur of the moment you have a reasonable chance of a seat. Membership is always necessary, so that the theatres can keep their club status, but the cost is usually nominal – around 50p, and as you can join at the door, this doesn't present any problem. The pubs usually open during normal hours, phone to check. Performances often start at *13.00* or *20.00*. For further details and times consult 'What's On & Where To Go' or 'Time Out'.

Bear and Staff, Cafe Theatre   **2** I 22
37 Charing Cross Rd (opposite Wyndham's Theatre) WC1. 01-240 0794. *Ind Coope.* Run by the Artaud

Theatre Company who create an amazing flow of entertainment with a minimum of one lunchtime and three evening shows. New plays and adaptations of novels and stories come to life from Mon through to Sun. You may take snacks or drinks in from the bar with you. **B.** *Theatre Mon–Sun.*

Bush Theatre
Bush Hotel, Shepherds Bush Green W12. 01-740 0501. *Taylor Walker*. The theatre, with its curtainless stage and raked seating, is above the pub. Established to attract the non-theatre-going public, its new productions often transfer to the West End. **B.** *Theatre Tue–Sun.*

Crown and Castle
600 Kingsland Rd E8. 01-254 3678. *Watneys*. Go up to the big Club Room on a Saturday night from *20.00* for late-night alternative comedy. Informal and fun with at least three acts to enjoy. *Theatre Sat only.*

Finborough Arms   4 J 5
118 Finborough Rd SW10. 01-373 3842. *Whitbread*. The Finborough Theatre Club offers new plays, some by the resident writer, though new scripts with local relevance are always considered. Stay after the show on Fri and Sat for alternative cabaret. Tasty bar snacks in the pub below. Priv rm. **B.** *Theatre Mon–Sat.*

Gate at the Prince Albert   1 A 8
11 Pembridge Rd W11. 01-229 0706. *Ind Coope*. One of the oldest of the pub theatres, specialising in new plays and the lesser-known works of important writers. After the show on Fri and Sat you sometimes get a topical satirical revue, and there are frequent late night cabarets. Pub below will quench your thirst but not feed you. *Theatre Mon–Sat.*

King's Head   3 E 32
115 Upper St N1. 01-226 1916. *Ind Coope*. Probably the best known and most widely reviewed of theatre pubs. The theatre is at the back of the one bar. It is fitted out with tables and chairs, so you can order the set meal – usually roast and two veg – then stay at your table for the play (lunchtime and evening). After the

performance, stick around for live music – folk rock on Mon, Tue & Wed, variety night on Thur & Fri, and rock on Sat eve. Theatre and restaurant closed on Sun but pub open usual hours and live jazz begins about *21.00*. **L D** *(Reserve)*. *Closed* **L D** *Sun. Theatre Mon–Sat.*

Latchmere Theatre   **4** R   6
503 Battersea Park Rd SW11. 01-228 2620. *Watneys.* Opened in 1982, above a real ale pub, this one has already established a good reputation for plays, cabaret and reviews. There is also a theatre bar. Check listings for late-night shows and Sunday performances. Outdoor beer garden and barbecue fare to eat all-year round. **B.** *Theatre Mon–Sat.*

Man in the Moon   **5** L 14
392 King's Rd SW3. 01-351 2876. *Watneys.* Possibly the most comfortable pub theatre in London – a purpose-built studio space with upholstered seating on two levels. Enterprising management presents predominantly modern plays – two different productions each night. The pub itself is worth a visit in its own right – lovely engraved glass, real ale, a gas log fire and lunchtime snacks. **B.** *Theatre Tue–Sat.*

Old Red Lion   **6** J 29
418 St John's St EC1. 01-837 7816. *Charrington.* Studio theatre upstairs which can seat 70. Watch evening performances of new and exciting plays. Downstairs, a large bar attracting plenty of passing trade, since the pub stands on a right of way. Home-cooked food lunchtime and evening. Pleasant back patio. **B.** *Theatre Tue-Sun.*

Orange Tree
45 Kew Rd, Richmond, Surrey. 01-940 3633. *Youngs.* Early Victorian building adorned with leaded windows and marble columns. The interior has plush chairs and carpets, inlaid mirrors, prints and paintings. In the theatre upstairs, which seats 80, the Orange Tree Theatre gives evening performances from Sep to Apr and rehearsed play readings during May. There are occasional productions for children and schools.

Downstairs in the cellar is a comfortable restaurant, with old panelling, brick walls and Spanish wrought-iron fittings, offering European food. Good quality and good value. **L D** *(Reserve* **D***). Closed* **L D** *Sun. Theatre Mon–Sat.*

Three Horseshoes
Heath St NW3. 01-435 3648. *Trumans.* Friendly pub serving snacks through till *20.30.* In the Club Room upstairs (no membership necessary) there is live folk once a week from Sep–Jun. The Pentameters put on plays and poetry readings here from time to time and post up their programmes in the bar. **B.** *Theatre irregular times.*

The Water Rats   **3** G 27
328 Gray's Inn Rd WC1. 01-837 7269. *Courage.* This ancient inn is now the home of the Abadaba Music Hall which hires professional actors to present lively, sometimes bawdy, modern music hall, pantomime and sing songs. Booking essential – ring the pub, or the company itself on 01-722 5395. There's also live music from Sun–Wed (no need to book) and varied 'hot dishes' to sustain you. **B. £.** *Music hall Thur–Sat.*

GAY PUBS _____

There are some London pubs that cater to an almost exclusively gay clientele, although most welcome 'straight' customers as well, unless they come to sneer or feel superior. Gay and drag pubs have been combined because while not all gay pubs offer drag acts, all pubs with drag acts attract an at least partially gay clientele. (For further information contact Gay Switchboard, 01-837 7324.)
Many of the pubs listed are frequented exclusively by male gays. In the gay world just as much as in the straight, the pub tends still to be a bit of a male preserve and gay women are more likely to meet in clubs. However, this is a state of affairs which seems to be changing gradually and one or two pubs where gay

women do congregate are mentioned below. Usual pub hours are kept unless otherwise stated.

Black Cap   **3** A 25
171 Camden High St NW1. 01-485 1742. *Charrington*. Originally built as a courthouse, hence the rather formidable name. Now mainly a male preserve of a different kind. Two bars, one with a pictorial history of the pub in tiles, the other decorated with photographs of famous drag acts. This second bar offers drag shows every night of the week and also at Sun lunchtime. Gay women also welcome. Pub doesn't open until *12.30* at lunchtime and *18.30* in the evening.

Brief Encounter   **5** J 22
41 St Martin's Lane WC2. 01-240 2221. A favourite West End pub. Downstairs there is live piano music every evening. Very crowded at pre-theatre and pre-night club times, but has a good atmosphere. Outdoor drinking on the pavement in summer. No food these days.

Champion   **1** A 8
1 Wellington Ter W11. 01-229 5056. *Charrington*. Large bar with snuggery leading out of it. Frequented by a lively crowd. Taped music. Popular with male gay locals. Occasional live entertainment including drag shows. **B.**

Comptons   **2** I 22
53 Old Compton St W1. 01-437 4445. *Charrington*. Large Soho pub with comfortable seating, friendly staff and substantial bar snacks at every session. **B.**

Fallen Angel
65 Grayham St N1. 01-253 3996. *Free House*. Trendy Islington pub which also functions as a vegetarian café. Tue is a very popular women-only night. The smartly refurbished bar holds regular exhibitions by gay and lesbian artists. **B.**

George IV
7a Ida St E14. 01-515 7339. *Watneys*. Amateur dramatic productions take place here once a month, intermingled with drag cabaret every Fri and Sat.

Large bar with pool table and definitely clubby atmosphere. Hot food and coffee is available at all times. **B.**

Goldsmith's Tavern
36 New Cross Rd SE14. 01-692 3648. *Courage*. A lively pub that is fast building a reputation for its disco, drag and alternative cabaret nights. Wed, Fri and Sat are the nights for gay-oriented cabaret. **B.**

King William IV
77 High St, Hampstead NW3. 01-435 5747. *Courage*. Traditional Hampstead pub with one large oak-panelled bar and a beer garden out at the back – cemented but made pretty with wall boxes full of trailing plants and an engaging mural. Predominantly male gay. Good taped music and tempting buffet, that often amounts to full meals. Speciality party nights in summer. In fine weather, there's a barbecue in the back garden on Fri and Sat. **B.**

London Apprentice   6 J 32
333 Old St EC1. 01-739 5577. *Free House*. Originally an American-style pub, which led the development of London's gay scene. Two large bars, plus dance floor, pool table, and videos everywhere. Attracts a predominantly male gay crowd. **B.** *Food at lunchtime only. Open Mon–Thur to 02.00; Fri & Sat to 03.00; Sun to 24.00.*

Queen's Head   4 L 11
27 Tryon St SW3. 01-589 0262. *Courage*. In a small side street near the beginning of the King's Road, and a good place to take some Dutch courage on board before plunging in among the medley of boutiques and shoe shops. Ground floor divided into three bars, which makes for cosier drinking. Modern decor with juke-box, fruit machine and video games. Almost entirely gay – both men and women welcome. **B.**

Royal Oak
Glenthorne Rd, Hammersmith W6. 01-748 2781. *Trumans*. Large art-deco pub with entertainment seven nights a week and Sun lunchtime. **B.** *Open Sun 12.00–16.00 for lunch and show. Sun–Thur to 24.00; Fri & Sat to 01.00.*

Royal Vauxhall Tavern

372 Kennington Lane SE11. 01-582 0833. *Courage*. Noisy, friendly pub which was the first in London to produce regular drag shows. Still puts them on, seven nights a week and at Sun lunchtime, on a stage at one end of the large brown and gold bar. When the acts aren't on (weekday lunchtime or early eve) the jukebox is, loudly! Mostly male gays and a few tourists. **B.** *Open to 24.00 Tue & Wed, to 02.00 Thur–Sat. Closed weekday mornings.*

Ship and Whale

2 Gulliver St SE16. 01-237 3305. *Trumans*. This building went up at the turn of the century, but there has been a pub here since 1664. Used to be used by whalers – and in the year of its first opening an actual whale made it this far up the Thames. Now, a totally male gay pub. There's a games room, with pool table and electronic games; a large horseshoe bar with a dance floor to one side; and a garden bar. The garden is concrete but there are flowers in pots and flood-lighting at night. Disco every night, and also Sun lunchtime. **B.** *Open to 24.00 Mon–Thur, to 02.00 Fri & Sat.*

Two Brewers

114 Clapham High St SW 4. 01-622 3621. *Charrington*. Big on entertainment with cabaret and drag shows Mon, Wed and Thur evening and a male stripper at Sun lunchtime. Snacks in the evenings only, very quiet at lunchtime. **B.**

BARS

The cult of the cocktail, whose revival was at a zenith when the previous Pub Guide was written, is still with us, but another trend is coming along very nicely beside it, and to a certain extent overlapping with it – the rise of the Continental-style brasserie.

While brasseries usually serve cocktails, cocktail bars

rarely serve meals and never offer breakfast and the daily papers. The brasserie, then, tends to be a place to go to any time of the day or evening, for whatever refreshment is appropriate to the moment, while the cocktail bar comes into its own at lunchtime and at the true cocktail hour in the evening. By the same token the brasserie is usually a more unorthodox place, stylish probably, but not formal. However, they seem to be learning from each other and the one thing common to both is that London's developing 'Café Society' goes to either one as much to make a statement as to buy a drink. The bar or brasserie is the stage on which the customers can pose, and the specific bar chosen, and the clothes worn to attend it, are all part of the enjoyable ritual of posing. That is not to say that the rest of us can't have a very nice time in any of the places listed below.

Of the cocktail bars, those run by the large West End hotels are still the most reliable. They also include in their number some of the most opulent and famous of them all. Cocktails are expensive but you do get value for money, glamorous surroundings, quality glass and bar staff with the expertise to concoct something to suit your personal taste.

Many of the brasseries are relatively new, but all those included here have got their act together. Their character and ambience is so individual that there is almost certainly one that is perfect for each potential customer.

Unless otherwise stated the bars listed in this chapter keep normal pub opening times.

American Bar 6 K 23

Savoy Hotel, Strand WC2. 01-836 4343. Sophisticated and snazzy with an enormous range of expertly mixed cocktails. Savoy 90, Royal Silver and Moonwalk are just three of the hotel's specials, and new ones are devised for special events. A pianist and singer entertains from Mon to Sat evenings. To drink here is to drink in style, and as you waver past the bookstall don't forget to buy the Savoy Cocktail Book to show you how to do it at home.

Athenaeum Bar   **2 I 18**
Athenaeum Hotel, Piccadilly W1. 01-499 3464.
Mellow wood-panelled room for discreet drinking.
The bar has London's largest selection of single malt
whiskies. The cocktail list includes all the classics but
the bar staff really prefer to provide what people ask
for.

Bar Escoba   **1 I 7**
102 Old Brompton Rd SW7. 01-373 2403. There are
plenty of seats on the pavement and two spacious
rooms within in this Spanish-style bar with its Mexican
beer and Tapas snacks. It may be mock Spanish, but
the effect is good – casual and friendly, and extra-lively
on Wed and Sun evenings when the flamenco dancers
flourish their all. *Open Mon–Sat 11.00–23.00; Sun
11.00–22.00*

Bill Stickers   **2 H 22**
18 Greek St W1. 01-437 0582. An amazing restaurant
and bar with fascinatingly over-the-top decor. They
serve about 30 different cocktails plus beer and wine.
Very popular with the famous – Bowie, Jagger,
Culture Club to name a few. *Open Mon–Fri
12.00–03.00; Sat 18.00–03.00; Sun 18.00–23.00.*

Bohemian Bar and Montego Bay   **5 K 12**
Chelsea Hotel, Sloane St SW1. 01-235 4377. Rich gold
and brown decor in the Bohemian Bar, overlooking a
Caribbean style swimming pool. Laze back in
comfortable leather armchairs and sip classic cocktails.
Or wander to Montego Bay, closer to the pool, to drink
Caribbean Coolers (banana dacquiri, perhaps) and
nibble tropical titbits. Don't panic, but in good
weather the roof comes off Montego Bay.

Bracewell's Bar   **2 I 18**
Park Lane Hotel, Piccadilly W1. 01-499 6321. So
popular that it has had to be extended to accommodate
all those wishing to partake of its competitively priced
and classic cocktails. Canapes, elegant supper snacks,
warm and friendly ambiance.

Braganza   **2 H 22**
56 Frith St W1. 01-437 5412. Brasserie below the

Braganza Restaurant – cool and pretty grey and white decor with pink touches, a bit like an upmarket hairdressers. Huge doors between café and pavement fold right back in summer. You need to be young and narrow to sit on the spindly chairs but the snacks – and especially the ice creams – are appealing enough to enlarge the outline. Cocktails, wines and champagne – and coffee and croissant at breakfast time. *Open Mon–Sat 09.00–23.30; Sat 18.00–23.30; Sun closed.*

Café Pelican 5 J 22
45 St Martin's Lane WC2. 01-379 0309. Usefully placed between the Lumiere Cinema and the Coliseum and more or less opposite the Duke of York's Theatre. Immensely long bar with a strong French accent and a 30s slant – bentwood chairs, marble tables, parlour palms. There are seats in an elegant little corral on the pavement out front. Continental breakfasts, cocktails, hot chocolate and light meals. *Open Mon–Sat 11.00–23.00; Sun 12.00–22.30.*

Cavalry Bar 2 I 14
Hyde Park Hotel, Knightsbridge SW1. 01-235 2000. Go through the Grill Room entrance to this lively bar with its military theme. A drum hangs from the ceiling and cavalry prints line the walls, but the lighting is soft, the canapes tasty and Charles's cocktails faultless. Whisky Sour and Bloody Mary are specially popular, but the Hyde Park Fizz goes down well, too.

Champagne Exchange 2 I 17
17c Curzon St W1. 01-493 4490. An elegant bar featuring an extensive wine list with over 40 different varieties of champagne. Appetising snacks can be enjoyed in the bar or visit the restaurant. *Closed Sun.*

Churchill Bar 2 D 17
Churchill Hotel, Portman Sq W1. 01-486 5800. Beautiful bar in a Regency-style room. The specially commissioned murals of Oriental sporting scenes blend subtly with the deep red fittings. Devilish Bloody Marys, very dry martinis and an impressive Churchill No 10 Special. Popular with diplomats and businessmen.

Cocktail Bar, Café Royal   **2** H 20
Café Royal, Regent St W1. 01-437 9090. Famous for
being grand and luxurious, and for the fact that Oscar
Wilde, Aubrey Beardsley and their ilk were regulars in
their day, the Café Royal has recently been
refurbished by Trust House Forte into an image of
itself a hundred years ago. A superb range of cocktails
and alcoholic coffees are presented in the Bar and the
Café Wilde is becoming established as a brasserie with
drinks, snacks and ambitious platters available. Both
have access to the superb wine cellars of the Café
Royal. *Open Mon–Sat 12.00–23.30; Sun 12.00–22.30.*

Criterion Brasserie   **2** I 20
222 Piccadilly Circus W1. 01-839 7133. If you dreamed
you dwelt in marble halls, this could have been the
place. No outlook, but the inlook is neo-Byzantine
marble splendour with pillared, mirrored walls and a
gold mosaic ceiling. Very spacious though it fills up at
lunch and theatre-supper time. Breakfast until *11.00*;
café-bar-style menu from *11.00–18.00*; Brasserie
menu at traditional meal times. It is a fashionable and
luxurious place to drink and eat. *Open Mon–Sat
08.00–23.30; Sun 10.00–22.30.*

The Dôme   **5** L 14
354 King's Rd SW3. 01-352 7611. A converted pub
named after the famous Paris Dôme. The café society
elite tend to sneer – perhaps because it's part of a chain
of four and so cannot be called unique. Ignore adverse
comments – the Dômes are amiable, friendly, popular
and provide good food, coffee, cocktails and most
other drinks at appropriate times throughout the day
to a thronging mixture of people. *Open Mon–Sat
09.00–23.00; Sun 10.00–22.30.*
Also at:
341 Upper St, Islington N1. 01-226 3414.   **3** E 32
38–39 Hampstead High St NW3. 01-435 4240.
Seacoal Lane EC4. 01-248 3741   **6** L 28

Drummonds of Chelsea   **5** L 14
49 King's Rd SW3. 01-730 8180. *Charrington*. This,
too, is one of a chain of successful pub conversions,

whose hallmarks are wide windows, parlour palms,
permanent background music, little marble tables and
sometimes sofas, and the odd chaise longue. They
serve good food all day, whether you want a meal or a
snack and offer coffees, cocktails and a wide range of
imported lagers and beers including Lamot and
Budweiser, as well as Bass. *Open Mon–Sun
09.30–23.00.*
Also at:
744 High Rd, Finchley N12. 01-445 5956.
73–77 Euston Rd, St Pancras NW1.   **3** D 22
01-387 4566.
245–247 Baker St NW1. 01-935 7321   **2** D 18
202 Upper Richmond Rd, Putney SW15.
01-788 8190.

Freud's   **2** I 21
198 Shaftesbury Av WC2. 01-240 9932. Creep down
fire escape stairs into a kind of crypt with stone walls,
slate floors and incomprehensible artwork on the
walls. The piano is played Mon, Wed and Fri
lunchtimes, otherwise the funky taped music takes
over. Sandwiches, salads, coffees, drinks, bottled
beers, newspapers; reasonable prices – but you need to
be young and able to cope with being where it's at.
Open Mon–Sat 11.00–23.00. Closed Sun.

Grabowski Gallery   **4** K 11
86 Sloane Av SW3. 01-589 4627. This really is an art
gallery – no need to pose here, the pictures on the
walls, all for sale, will do it for you. The food – light and
imaginative – is on at lunchtime only, the rest of the
time you may drink wine when licensing laws permit,
and coffee and soft drinks when they don't. Pleasant,
cultured atmosphere – the garden with its fountain is
an added bonus. *Open Mon–Sat 11.00–23.00. Closed
Sun.*

Henry J Bean's   **4** L 4
(But His Friends All Call Him Hank)
195–197 King's Rd SW3. 01-352 9255. Once a
traditional pub called The Six Bells, the striking
frontage with its grinning demons now opens onto an
American bar and grill with a list of 25 house cocktails

and a variety of American beers. The snacks are of the nachos, chilli, chicken in a bun and fried potato skins type. Packed and friendly with a garden out the back. **B**. *Open Mon–Sat 11.30–23.00, licensed to 24.00; Sun open 12.00–22.30.* **£.**

Joe's Cafe   **4** K 11
126 Draycott Av SW3. 01-225 2217. Smartly done out in black, white and chrome with fresh white flowers and a plethora of waiters and waitresses in black with white aprons. Larger than it looks, on two levels, with the bar at the front and a couple of pavement tables. Short but nice wine list, two or three cocktails, breakfasts, original and interesting salads, and hot specials which might feature king prawns or steak. Very pleasant but not cheap. *Open Mon–Sat 09.30–23.30; Sun 11.00–14.30. Closed 18.00–19.00 Sat.*

Jules Bar   **2** J 19
85 Jermyn St SW1. 01-930 4700. The first free-standing cocktail bar in London. Chandeliers and plush red velvet upholstery echo the expensive club-like atmosphere. Huge variety of cocktails (Blue Lagoon and Jules Reviver are favourites), crisps in silver bowls and smoked salmon at the bar. *Pianist plays from 17.30–22.30 Mon–Fri. Closed Sun.*

Lillie Langtry Bar   **5** K 12
Cadogan Hotel, Sloane St SW1. 01-235 7141. Charming, intimate cocktail lounge in the building where the 'Jersey Lily' entertained. The decor is aptly Edwardian, with delicate colours and feminine elegance.

Old Rangoon
201 Castlenau SW13 01-741 9655. *Courage.* A beautiful bar and restaurant in this handsome colonial-style building with a lovely secluded garden behind. Here you can sit and watch the ducks while sipping an exotic cocktail or enjoy a meal in the restaurant. Afternoon teas also available. **B L D.** **££.**

Palm Court   **2** I 18
The Ritz, Piccadilly W1. 01-493 8181. Designed by

Cesar Ritz himself, this splendid baroque room with its central gold leaf fountain is redolent with nostalgia for a bygone era. Mr Michael presides over the cocktails. Still popular is the vodka or gin Ricci – synonymous with the Ritz in the cocktail bar heyday. Has always been a rendezvous for visiting celebrities.

The Pheasantry   **5** L 14
152 King's Rd SW3. 01-351 3084. A modest 19th-century house with an over-dramatic entrance arch. It became famous from the 30s to the 60s as a club frequented by Dylan Thomas, Diaghilev, Augustus John and others, and was snatched away from the jaws of the developers in the 70s. It reopened in 1982 as a brasserie and cocktail bar serving spritzers and espressos to smart King's Road types. Brunch menu in the daytime, dinner menu at night. *Open Mon–Sat 12.00–23.00; Sun 12.30–22.00.*

Piano Bar   **2** G 16
Dorchester Hotel, Park Lane W1. 01-629 8888. Classic, well-mixed cocktails and tempting early evening canapes in the ceramic, glass and mirror lined room. Light lunches and suppers are also available. Every evening a pianist entertains on the grand piano that gives this stylish bar its name. *Licensed to 24.00.*

Polo Bar   **2** E 18
Coconut Grove, 3–5 Barrett St W1. 01-486 5269. Owned by the Peppermint Park people, this is a 'deco-flavoured' touch of old Hollywood with mirrored walls, masses of plants and a glittery clientele. International selection of cocktails includes their own Coconut Carnival, Rangoon Rugby and Slimmers. Cocktails are also served in the restaurant famous for its gargantuan desserts.

Rebatos
169 South Lambeth Rd SW8. 01-235 6388. A taste of Spain south of the Thames. Rebatos is a bustling bar serving smooth Spanish wines, beers and a vast range of spirits. The tapas are extensive and authentic – tortilla, calamares, eel, chirizo. There is also a restaurant at the back – essential to reserve. *Closed Sun.*

Rib Room Bar   5 K 13

Carlton Tower Hotel, Cadogan Pl SW1. 01-235 5411.
Felix Topolski drawings and paintings line the walls of
this swish bar much frequented by the smart set. A
wide range of cocktails prepared by Ray Sese.
Particularly good dry Martinis.

Rumours   6 J 24

33 Wellington St WC2. 01-836 0038. Very much in the
chi-chi Covent Garden image. Large, pillared room
with an extensively stocked bar surrounded by mirrors.
A former flower market, now where the fashionable
enjoy an imaginative range of modern and classic
cocktails. Happy Hour, with cheaper drinks,
17.30–20.30 Fri & Sat and Sun–Thur all evening.

Smollensky's Balloon   2 I 19

1 Dover St W1. 01-491 1199. A bar and restaurant,
with live music nightly. Underground but classy with
much polished wood and a mirrored ceiling. There are
videos behind the bar, trompe l'oeil decorations on the
restaurant walls. Classic and de luxe cocktails, as well
as their own house inventions. Wine by the glass may
seem pricey, but the measure is huge. Definitely a bar
not a brasserie, though the restaurant does do
afternoon teas and also cares about children and
vegetarians. *Open Mon–Sat 12.00–23.45; Sun
12.00–22.30.*

Soho Brasserie   2 I 22

23–25 Old Compton St W1. 01-439 9301. Coffee and
drinks in the front, meals at the back, in this arty
French-style brasserie. It's a pub conversion and the
enormous bar somehow looks as if it's trying to push
the customers into the street – on fine days they submit
and sit with one foot on the pavement, happy to see
and be seen. *Open 11.00–23.00. Closed Sun.*

Trader Vic's   2 G 16

Hilton Hotel, Park Lane W1. 01-493 8000. A sultry
South Sea island setting complete with bamboo,
fishing nets and Hawaiian-shirted waiters. An
enormous range of exotic brews, many of them
rum-based, served in extravagant bowls, often with

flowers floating in them. Samoan Fog Cutter and The Scorpion are two of the killers. *Closed Sat lunchtime.*

Zona Rosa   **3** J 23
3 Long Acre WC2. 01-836 5255. Mexican cocktail bar and restaurant. Try one of the range of 15 different fruit-flavoured frozen Margaritas or a Mexican beer or something from the vast range of spirits. Food is available – Mexican specialities such as quesados and spicy chicken wings. **B L D**. *Open to 03.00; Sun to 24.00.* **££**.

WINE BARS _____

Wine bars have become a well-established alternative to pub drinking. They provide a relaxed, often candle-lit setting, where you can drink wine, eat, listen to music or just relax with friends. The better places carry a good range of well-known quality wines, a few unusual bottles and at least one reliable house number. Ports, sherries and madeiras are also generally available. As almost all wine bars offer wine by the glass, it is possible to taste a pleasing variety. Quiche, cheese, pâté and salad are typical wine bar foods, though a lot do go in for fuller meals, and some even have their own restaurants.
They are subject to the usual licensing laws, but sometimes operate like a brasserie and stay open all day serving food, soft drinks, coffee and afternoon tea while alcohol is withheld. Then again, they may close early if trade falls off. Assume the bars listed are open during normal pub hours unless otherwise stated.

CHARING CROSS RD, HOLBORN AND BLOOMSBURY

L'Almacas   **3** J 26
15 Leigh St WC1. 01-387 0040. Small and pretty with an attractive back garden with tables and a full-sized telephone box, should you want to call a friend or

change into Superman. French, Italian, German and Spanish wines and an interesting selection of food from steaks to vegetarian dishes, with seafood crêpes a speciality. **B L D**. *Open all day in summer. Closed* **L** *Sat & Sun.* **££.**

The Bunghole   3 I 23
57 High Holborn WC1. 01-242-4318. One of the Davy's chain – see **City** Section.

Fino's Wine Cellar   2 I 22
104 Charing Cross Rd WC2. 01-836 1077. Pleasant wine bar with theatrical embellishments – a large frameful of signatures of the famous, photographs of actors and dancers, and theatrical costumes hanging from ceiling and walls. Tasty buffet food and a restaurant serving Italian specialities. **B L D** *(Reserve). Closed Sat lunchtime & all Sun.* **££.**

The Old Bottlescrue   6 K 28
Bath House, Holborn Viaduct EC1. 01-248 2157. One of the Davy's chain – see **City** Section.

CHELSEA AND KNIGHTSBRIDGE

Bill Bentley's Wine Bar   2 I 12
31 Beauchamp Pl SW3. 01-589 5080. Dark, cosy, old-fashioned bar with an excellent fish restaurant upstairs. The wine, mostly good quality French, is reasonably priced and well accompanied by delicious snacks from the oyster bar. Lots of river pictures on the walls because Bill Bentley likes messing about in boats. Pleasant garden for summer drinking. **B L D** (Reserve **D**). *Closed Sun.* **££.**

Blushes Café   4 L 11
52 King's Rd SW3. 01-589 6640. French café-style wine bar on two levels. Pavement drinking in summer. Mirrored interior with lots of greenery. French, Italian and Mexican dishes are popular as is the traditional English breakfast. Live music at weekends. **B L D**. *Open all day and evening Mon–Sun.* **££.**

Charco's   4 L 11
1 Bray Pl SW3. 01-584 0765. Rustic in design with a

stable-like interior and walls covered in antique sugar moulds. Go down to the basement for dim lights and 18th century reproduction prints. More than 90 wines, interesting salads, game pies, seafood and the odd Russian special. Pavement tables in summer. **B.** *Closed Sun.*

Loose Box   **2 I 12**
7 Cheval Pl SW7. 01-584 9280. Ample, friendly and quite peaceful. Downstairs you can sit in stalls and contemplate the odd bridle hanging on the wall. There's a large buffet and 63 wines (17 by the glass), as well as port, sherry and Martini. Upstairs restaurant serves home-made English pub food. **B L D.** *Closed Sun.* **£.**

Maxie's   **2 H 13**
143 Knightsbridge SW1. 01-225 2553. Popular Knightsbridge wine bar with a carefully selected wine list and an original line in Chinese snacks – Peking Duck and spring rolls make a welcome change from the usual quiche. The separate restaurant area has a more extensive, and expensive, menu. **B L D.** *Closed Sun.* **£** or **££.**

Sloane's   **5 L 12**
52 Sloane Sq SW1. 01-730 4275. The Oriel stands on Sloane Square, and Sloane's wine bar spreads throughout its large cellars. Comfortable, candlelit and meandering, with a good range of wines, hefty snacks available plus a good range of salads, and a sprinkling of famous faces if you can spot them among all the rest. Food in the evening until *22.00.* Live jazz Tue to Thur eve. **B.**

The Wine Gallery   **4 K 6**
Hollywood Rd SW10. 01-352 7572. New venture from Samuel Courtauld's great-nephew and restaurateur John Brinkley, sited next to Brinkley's restaurant. They have created a wine bar-cum-art gallery where painters and photographers can show their work and the rest of us can drink good medium-priced wine, eat interesting snacks, and toy with the possibility of supporting the arts by buying a piece of the decor. **B.**

CLERKENWELL AND ISLINGTON

The Actor's Retreat
6 J 29

326 St John's St EC1. 01-837 0722. Popular
family-owned wine bar with restaurant, handy for
Sadler's Wells Theatre. Friendly and pretty with a
Sicilian-Italian ambience and food. Attractive ceramic
tiled walls, old beams, the original fireplace and
numerous photos of actors and actresses. Good range
of French, Spanish and Italian wines, crab and fresh
salmon in season, gateaux and ices. There is gentle
background music all the time and parties or events are
held sporadically throughout the year. **B L D** (*Reserve*
L D). *Closed L Sat, Sun* **L D**. **££** or **£££**.

Burgundy Ben's
3 I 28

102–108 Clerkenwell Rd EC1. 01-251 3783. One of the
Davy's chain – see **City** Section.

Café St Pierre
3 I 29

29 Clerkenwell Green EC1. 01-251 6606. Ground floor
brasserie is welcoming and airy with jazz-funk
background music, huge windows and mirrors, and
fresh flowers. Coffee, pastries, salads, good cheeses,
teas, well chosen wines, mussels (in season) in
mayonnaise and mustard. Winner of 'The Standard'
Wine Bar of the Year award, 1982. In the upstairs
restaurant try deep-fried camembert, turbot in white
wine sauce, rich sweets, port, brandy and cigars.
B L D. *Closed Sat & Sun*. **££** or **£££**.

THE CITY

Balls Bros

One of the oldest wine bar chains in London, run by a
firm of wine shippers and merchants. All their bars
serve the same sound selection of about 70 wines.
There are always good sandwiches and sometimes a
cold buffet. These City bars are rather like clubs, but
still friendly to newcomers. *Bars open Mon–Fri only,
11.00–1500; 17.00–19.30.*

3 Budge Row EC4. 01-248 7557   **6 N 29**
5 Carey Lane EC2. 01-606 4787   **6 L 29**

6 Cheapside EC2. 01-248 2708   **6 M 29**
Hay's Galleria, Tooley St SE1.   **6 Q 30**
01-407 4301. Has its own fish restaurant.
Laurence Poutney Hill EC4. 01-283 2947   **6 O 30**
Liverpool St EC2. 01-626 7919.   **6 N 33**
Moor House, London Wall EC2.   **6 L 31**
01-628 3944.
2 Old Change Ct EC4. 01-248 8697   **6 M 28**
St Mary at Hill EC3. 01-626 0321   **6 P 31**
42 Threadneedle St EC2. 01-283 6701.   **6 N 31**

Bill Bentley's Wine Bar   **6 N 32**
18 Old Broad St EC2. 01-588 2655. A veritable oasis in
the City, with its beautiful back garden overlooked by
an elegant verandah. There is a top quality fish
restaurant and an oyster bar, but if you don't want to
eat you may simply drink the reasonably-priced,
mostly French, wine, by glass or bottle. **B L** *(Reserve
L). Closes at 21.00 & all weekend.* **££** or **£££.**

Bow Wine Vaults   **6 M 29**
10 Bow Churchyard EC4. 01-248 1121. Victorian bar
not only within hearing of Bow Church Bells, but right
next to them! Popular with City gents, the bar offers a
fine selection of well chosen French, Spanish,
Californian and German wines. Sandwiches,
imaginative bar food. Lunchtime restaurant serves a
lot of game. Priv rm. **B L.** *Open to 19.00. Closed Sat &
Sun.* **£.**

The Broker   **6 Q 32**
16 Byward St EC3. 01-488 0131. Serves beers and
spirits as well as wines. Also has a cellar restaurant with
attendant cocktail bar. Usual snacks in the ground
floor wine bar, which is decorated with ornaments and
lamps from the old Lloyds building, saved by the
owner when the building was demolished. The original
cartoons and drawings are all for sale. **B L.** *Open to
20.00. Closed Sat & Sun.* **£.**

Corney and Barrow   **6 N 32**
109 Old Broad St EC2. 01-638 9308. Crowded City bar
and French restaurant. Good port from the cask,
plenty of wines – and spirits if you want a quick lift.

Cold buffet in the lower bar; immense variety of
sandwiches in the upper bar, with home-made fruit
cake to finish. **B L.** *Open Mon–Fri 11.30–15.00,
17.00–19.00. Closed Sat & Sun. Restaurant open
12.00–14.30 Mon–Fri.*

Davy's Wine Bars
Dusty barrels, old prints and sawdust-covered floors
create the Victorian image of these houses, most of
whose names relate to the wine trade of 100 years ago.
Six good house wines and a range of 24 more expensive
ones, together with a good choice of ports and sherries.
They all offer a cold buffet, freshly cut sandwiches and
cold fishy dishes – salmon, crab, lobster and so on. A
few serve steaks, savouries and puddings. *Most City
branches open from 11.00–15.00, 17.00–20.30,
Mon–Fri only. Other branches keep normal pub hours.*

Bangers   6 L 33
2/12 Wilson St EC2. 01-377 6326.

Bishop of Norwich   6 M 31
91/93 Moorgate EC2. 01-920 0857.

Bottlescrue   6 K 28
Bath House, 53/60 Holborn Viaduct EC1.
01-248 2157.

Burgundy Ben's   3 1 28
102/108 Clerkenwell Rd EC1. 01-251 3783.

City Boot   6 L 31
7 Moorfields High Walk EC2. 01-588 4766.

City Flogger   6 0 31
120 Fenchurch St EC3. 01-623 3251.

City F.O.B.   6 P 30
Lower Thames St EC3. 01-621 0619.

City Pipe   6 L 29
Foster Lane EC2. 01-606 2110.

City Vaults   6 L 29
2 St Martins-le-Grand EC1. 01-606 8721.

Colonel Jaspers   6 K 33
190 City Rd EC1. 01-608 0925.

Grapeshots
213 Artillery Pas, Bishopsgate E1. 01-247 8215.

The Habit   **6** P 32
Friary Court, 65 Crutched Friars EC3. 01-481 1137.

Mother Bunch's   **6** L 28
Old Seacoal Lane EC4. 01-236 5317.

The Pulpit   **6** L 33
Worship St EC2. 01-377 1574.

The Spittoon   **6** K 29
15/17 Long Lane EC1. 01-726 8858.

Udder Place   **6** M 30
Russia Court, Russia Row, 1/6 Milk St EC2.
01-600 2165.

The Vineyard Coffee House   **6** R 32
International House, 1 St Katharine's Way E1.
01-480 5088.

Five Lamps   **6** P 32
3 Railway Pl EC3. 01-488 1587. Next door to
Fenchurch St station. Basement bar, popular with
underwriters and brokers from nearby Lloyds. Good
selection of French, Italian and German wines. An old
marble bar at which to eat the hot and cold buffet. The
bar is bookable for groups. Upstairs bar for more wine,
spirits and beer as well. Run by Raymond, who makes
a point of welcoming his regulars by name. Priv rm. **B.**
Open to 20.00. Closed Sat & Sun.

Whittington's   **6** N 29
21 College Hill, Cannon St EC4. 01-248 5855. Popular
City bar in Dick Whittington's own vaulted wine
cellars. High proportion of regular customers. One of
the few wine bars with a full licence so you have a
choice between spirits or the reliable French, German
and Italian stock. Cold buffet and also separate à la
carte restaurant with enjoyable English and French
food. No food in the evening. **B L** *(Reserve). Open
Mon–Fri 11.30–15.00, 17.00–19.30.* **£££.**

COVENT GARDEN

Le Beaujolais   **2** I 22
25 Litchfield St WC2. 01-836 2277. Lively, mixed
clientele in a popular, intimate wine bar. Good French

wines, including their own-label house red and white and, of course, Beaujolais. Authentic French cooking. **L D.** *Closed* **L** *Sat & all Sun.* **££.**

Brahms and Liszt   **6** J 23
19 Russell St WC2. 01-240 3661. Particularly popular Covent Garden rendezvous. Lively, noisy and crowded. Loud taped music upstairs; live music downstairs in the evenings. Very reasonable selection of wines, hot and cold food. If you want to sit down at lunchtime you'll have to book. *Downstairs open to 01.00 Mon–Sat, to 22.30 Sun.* **B.**

Café des Amis du Vin   **6** J 23
12–13 Hanover Pl WC2. 01-379 3444. Bustling basement bar beneath the Brasserie which is itself beneath the elegant Salon des Amis du Vin Restaurant. Distinctly French flavour, with plainwood tables nudging each other. Boudin noir (French version of black pudding), plats du jour, chocolate truffles. Good range of French, Italian, Spanish and German wines. **L D** *(Reserve). Closed Sun.* **££** or **£££.**

The Crusting Pipe   **6** J 23
Unit 27, The Market WC2. 01-836 1415. One of the Davy chain – see **City** Section.

Penny's Place   **6** J 23
6 King St WC2. 01-836 4553. Converted pub with French ambience and predominantly Australian wine list. Downstairs is the VIP Bar, a French restaurant with fully licensed bar, cocktails, beers, spirits, the lot. Cover charge in restaurant. But both there and on the ground floor you can eat as little as a bowl of good soup or as much as a full meal. **B L D.** *Closed Sun.* **£** or **££.**

GREENWICH

Bar Du Musee
17 Nelson Rd SE10. 01-858 4710. Good place to stop for refreshment after a visit to the nearby National Maritime Museum, as the name suggests. Small and attractive, with a garden, a brief but sensible wine list and the usual food. **B.**

Colonel Jaspers
161 Greenwich High Rd SE10. 01-853 0585. One of the
Davy chain – see **City** Section.

Davy's Wine Vaults
165 Greenwich High Rd SE10. 01-858 7204. One of the
Davy chain – see **City** Section.

HOLLAND PARK AND NOTTING HILL

Julie's Bar   1 A   5
137 Portland Rd W11. 01-727 7985. Downstairs there's
a wooden bar with mirrors. Upstairs an intimate,
informal lounge with a mixture of sofas and Moroccan
furniture and a small glassed-over balcony piled with
Persian rug cushions. Serves proper cream teas when
the bar is closed between *16.00 and 18.00;* also
traditional Sun lunch. Mostly French wines. Hot dishes
or salads always available. **B L D. ££** or **£££.**

One Nine Two   1 A   8
192 Kensington Park Rd W11. 01-229 0482. This is
where the Notting Hill chic hang out. Simple decor
upstairs and down, but has an excellent French
restaurant and a predominantly French wine list with
several champagnes. You don't have to eat, and you
can choose one dish or fill yourself on a full
three-course meal. Either way, there's a superb
cheeseboard to accompany the wine. **L D.** *Closed Sun
eve.* **££.**

KENSINGTON

Drinks   1 E   6
21 Abingdon Rd W8. 01-937 6504. True to its name –
you can call in just for a drink – though the menu may
well prove too attractive to overlook. Elegant,
polished, definitely up-market but not overpriced –
except, possibly, if you order wine by the glass. *Closed
Sun.* **£** or **££.**

Jimmie's Wine Bar   1 D   8
18 Kensington Church St W8. 01-937 9988. The bar has
moved down the road from its original premises, in the

old stables of Kensington Barracks, but has retained its former ambience. Notable clarets and a wide range of food, including home-made sausages and fresh vegetables every day. Live music in the evenings, mostly light rock or pop. **B L D** *(Reserve)*. **£** or **££.**

No 1   **1 D   4**
Kensington High St W8. 01-937 0393. One of the Davy chain – see **City** Section. *Closed Sun.*

Scandies   **1 F   7**
4 Kynance Pl SW7. 01-589 3659. Intimate and very friendly with a connoisseurs list of wines and interesting food – Stilton pâté, smoked chicken salad, salmon steaks and a home-made special every day. Often full, but there's more room downstairs. **B L D. £.**

NORTH LONDON

Almeida Theatre Wine Bar   **3 D 33**
1a Almeida St N1. 01-226 0931. The Almeida, though perhaps best known for its annual contemporary music festival, also presents touring productions of a young and innovative kind. The wine bar can be enjoyed as well as, or instead of, the theatre. Interesting stock of wines, by bottle or glass, usually one guest beer, excellent food, extra special puddings. **B.** *Closed Sun.* **£.**

Boos Wine Bar   **2 A 18**
1 Glentworth St NW1. 01-935 3827. Friendly wine bar on two floors, named for a town in France. Serves French, Spanish, Italian and Australian wines and substantial home-made snacks – mousses, quiches, pies, salads. In winter, try the hot dish of the day. **B.** *Open to 20.00. Closed Sat & Sun.*

Champagne Charlies
325 Essex Rd N1. 01-226 4078. One of the Davy chain – see **City** Section.

Pinot's
34 Rosslyn Hill NW3. 01-435 5203. Crowded French café-like wine bar. Overflow to the pavement, or down

to the spacious Cellar Bar. Wide range of medium priced wines from France, Germany, Italy, Yugoslavia and Hungary, and some unusual bottled lagers. Good choice of 'real' food – coquille au gratin, fish pie, moussaka, chilli, vegetarian dish of the day. Live music most evenings. **B L D. £.**

PADDINGTON AND MARYLEBONE

Gyngleboy   **2** B 13
27 Spring St W2. 01-723 3351. One of the Davy chain – see **City** Section.

Lantern   **2** B 16
22 Harcourt St W1. 01-402 5925. Wine bar and bistro on two floors of a Georgian terraced house; rustic and romantic. Good range of French, Italian and German wines and a few bottled lagers. The food is home-made and English – soups, salads, pies. Gentle taped music. **B L D** (Reserve). *Closed Sat & Sun (except for private functions).* **£.**

SOUTH LONDON

Archduke   **6** M 23
Concert Hall Approach SE1. 01-928 9370. Built into a railway arch with natural brickwork, bright red overhead pipes and plenty of vegetation in hanging baskets. On first two levels – salads, quiches and cheesecake are available as well as a good range of wines. Upstairs restaurant serves sausages – made to recipes from all over the world – and a range of other foods. Very friendly service, live jazz and blues nightly. **B L D** (Reserve). *Closed Sat lunchtime & all Sun.* **££.**

The Boot and Flogger   **6** Q 27
10–20 Redcross Way SE1. 01-407 1184. One of the Davy's chain – see **City** Section.

Frog's Legs   **4** R 8
264 Battersea Park Rd SW11. 01-228 3794. Predominantly French wines and although much of the

food is of a home-made English type, you can always get bread-crumbed frog's legs. Nice unhurried French ambience. **B L D.** *Closed Sun.* **££.**

The Guinea Butt   6 Q 28
Chaucer House, White Hart Yard SE1. 01-407 2829. One of the Davy chain – see **City** Section.

Pitcher and Piano   4 L 4
871–873 Fulham Rd SW6. 01-736 3910. Pleasant, light and airy with plenty of room to sit down. A jazz piano plays Mon, Wed, Fri & Sun eves. Brief but well chosen wine list – short but regularly changed menu – avocado filled with crab in season, monkfish and fresh vegetables, home-made puddings. **B L D. ££.**

Stinkers   6 Q 30
42 Tooley St SE1. 01-407 9189. One of the Davy's chain – see **City** Section.

STRAND AND FLEET STREET

El Vino   6 K 26
47 Fleet St EC4. 01-353 6786. Something of an institution; musty atmosphere and thoroughly masculine (you even get mustard in your egg

El Vino wine bar

mayonnaise sandwich). Regular haunt of lawyers and journalists, who are requested to wear jacket, collar and tie at all times. Ladies were not permitted to buy drinks at the bar until 1982. Long impressive list of French and German wines and about ten varieties of champagne. Cold food restaurant in the cellar. Has an off-licence open from *09.00–20.00.* Priv rm. **B L** *(Reserve). Closed Sat eve & all Sun.* **£.**

Gordon's Wine Cellar   **5 K 22**
47 Villiers St WC2. 01-930 1408. 300-year-old cellar hidden in Watergate Walk. A main bar and a tunnel-shaped inner sanctum. Only Quasimodo could be truly comfortable, hunched against the damp curvature of the ancient stone walls, yet the candlelit atmosphere is so pleasant that customers return again and again. Particularly good selection of sherries, ports and madeiras. Very good cold buffet, and hot meals in winter. **B.** *Open to 21.00. Closed Sat & Sun.*

The Tappit Hen   **5 J 22**
5 William IV St, Strand WC2. 01-836 9839. One of the Davy's chain – see **City** Section.

Wine Press   **6 K 26**
161 Fleet St EC4. 01-353 9550. Bit different from the usual Fleet Street watering hole, which tends to be dark and masculine. Here there is light wood, bent-wood chairs, garden furniture, lots of cane, amber screens in front of the windows – and women are welcomed rather than tolerated. Bar snacks and 60 European wines. Two-thirds of the bar is set up as a good but pricey restaurant. **B L D** *(Reserve). Closed Sat & Sun.* **££.**

VICTORIA AND PIMLICO

Alexanders   **5 O 18**
37 Horseferry Rd SW1. 01-834 2907. One huge room with a cocktail bar and à la carte restaurant, serving predominantly French and Italian food, at one side, and a wine bar and buffet at the other. Extensive wine list, regular 'promotions' when a selected wine is cheap, beer and spirits, too. Occasional live big-band

music and a disco every Fri night. Sat night is party
night, with live entertainers, a disco and fast food. **B L
D.** *Closed Sat lunchtime & all Sun.* **£** or **££.**

Ebury Wine Bar   **5** M 13
139 Ebury St SW1. 01-730 5447. Long, narrow, calm
sort of bar done out in green and eggshell with cane
chairs and old sewing maching tables. Not cheap.
Comprehensive wine list, full à la carte lunches and
dinners. Sporadic live entertainment of a musical
persuasion. **L D** *(Reserve).* **££.**

Methuselah's Wine Bar   **5** M 16
29 Victoria St SW1. 01-222 3550. This friendly,
pleasant wine bar won the 1986 'Standard' Wine Bar of
the Year title. In partnership with the Cork and Bottle,
it offers the same wide range of very competitively
priced wines from all over the world and a delicious hot
and cold buffet. Obviously a successful combination.
B.

The Tapster   **5** L 17
3 Brewers Green, Buckingham Gate SW1. 01-222
0561. One of the Davy's chain – see **City** Section.

WEST END

Andrew Edmunds   **2** H 21
46 Lexington St W1. 01-437 5708. Attractive Soho
wine bar opened by the owner of the print gallery next
door. Excellent selection of French wines, plus port
and six champagnes. There is no background music;
instead the atmosphere hums with conversation from
the densely packed tables. The menu changes daily and
offers some of the best wine bar food in London. Ham
and brie in a hot baguette, pasta parcels stuffed with
spinach and ricotta, delicious salads. **B L D** *(Reserve).*
Closed Sat & Sun. **£.**

Chopper Lump   **2** G 19
10c Hanover Sq W1. 01-499 7569. One of the Davy
chain – see **City** Section. *Closed Sun.*

Cork and Bottle   **5** J 22
44–6 Cranbourn St WC2. 01-734 7807. Spacious

basement, its walls covered with framed prints and posters about wines and wine-growing areas, and its racks carrying more than 150 top-class bargains – including some from New Zealand to match the owner. Excellent salads, hot dishes and desserts. Lots of publishing and theatre people foregather here. 1984 'Standard' Wine Bar of the Year. **B.**

Downs   2 I 17
5 Down St W1. 01-491 3810. Sleek Mayfair bar on two levels. Upstairs is for drinking only, or snacks; downstairs is a proper restaurant. The disco, with DJ and dancing, is free, though you must have a meal. Open to midnight but after *23.00* the licensing laws say you must eat. Good range of French wines. **B L D** *(Reserve). Open to 24.00.* **£** or **££.**

Dover Street Wine Bar   2 I 19
8–9 Dover St W1. 01-629 9813. The speciality of the house in this large basement bar is the top quality live music, predominantly jazz but some soul and blues too, played six nights a week from 22.00. Good range of wines and an à la carte restaurant lunchtime and evening. *Open to 03.00 Mon–Sat. Closed Sun.* **B L D. £** or **££.**

Shampers   2 H 20
4 Kingly St W1. 01-437 1692. A wide range of wines on offer from all over the world. Lots of champagne drunk here (appropriately enough) perhaps because there are 53 advertising agencies within walking distance. Interesting French wall posters and taped jazz. Tasty hot and cold buffet upstairs and down. Convenient for the Shaftesbury Avenue theatres. **B.** *Closed Sat eve & Sun.*

Solange's Wine Bar   5 J 22
11 St Martin's Court WC2. 01-240 0245. A large wine bar decorated in the style of a traditional French brasserie with outside drinking on the pavement in summer. Very handy to the theatres and cinemas of Leicester Square and Charing Cross Road. There is a good selection of wines that can be sampled by the glass, and a menu of the day is available plus a good

range of cold meats and salads. **B.** *Open to 23.45 Mon–Sat. Closed Sun.*

Tracks   2 H 22
Soho Sq W1. 01-439 2318. Pine furnishings, plants and paintings inside. Continental-style terrace for drinking outside in summer. The wide selection of wines comes from 16 countries. Open all day and evening – serving breakfast, coffee, food and afternoon tea when the bar is closed. Popular with the nearby film industry. **B.** *Open Mon–Fri 10.00–23.00. Closed Sat & Sun (except for private parties).* **£.**

The Warren   2 D 22
Fitzroy Court, off Tottenham Court Rd. W1. 01-388 4131. Aptly named, this dimly-lit, subterranean wine bar is approached by iron steps. Imaginative food – always two hot dishes which change daily and a selection of salads. French, German, Spanish, Portuguese and Italian wines. Immensely popular, especially at lunchtimes. **B.** *Closed Sat daytime & all Sun.*

Wilfred's Wine Bar   6 L 25
Embankment WC2. 01-379 5496. This old Thames sailing barge moored across the road from the Temple Underground station has been converted into a unique wine bar. Good food and wines available. Wilfred's may be hired by private parties so it is advisable to phone and check whether or not it is open to the public at a particular time. **B.** *Closed Sun eve.*

Wolsey's Wine Bar   2 F 21
52 Wells St W1. 01-636 5121. Friendly and rather up-market wine bar above the pub of the same name. Good cold buffet, with one hot dish of the day, and wines from France, California, New Zealand and Australia. There are regular exhibitions of pictures by contemporary artists, all for sale, and occasional live jazz in the evenings. **B.** *Closed Sat & Sun.* **£.**

Index

MAPS

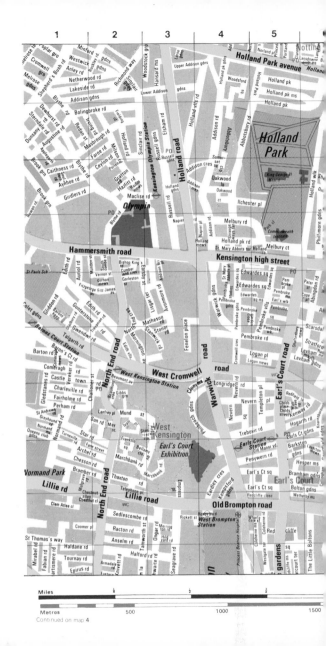

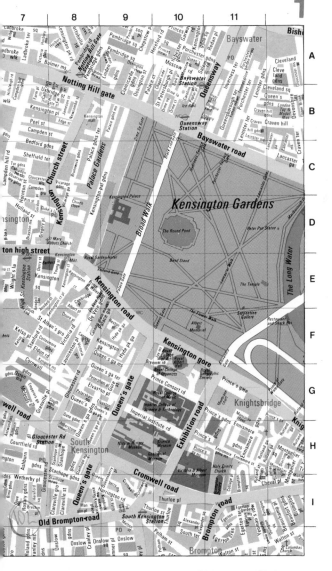

7   8   9   10   11

A
B
C
D
E
F
G
H
I

Ladbroke   Willing   Kensington pk rd   sq   Pembridge sq   Chepstow rd   Hereford rd   Princes sq   Garway rd   Kensington   Redan pl   **Bayswater**   **Bish**
Ladbroke ter   Bulmer ms   Notting Hill Gate   Pembridge gdns   Pembridge sq   Dawson pl   Moscow rd   Princes mews   Porchester gdns   Inverness ter   Queensway   PO   Cleveland   Cleve land   Cleveland sq
wlk   Hillsleigh rd   Campden hill rd   Uxbridge st   **Notting Hill gate**   Palace gardens ter   Linden gdns   St Petersburgh   pl   Moscow rd   Ossington st   Palace ct   Bayswater Station   Ice Rink   Queensborough ter   Porchester ter   Leinster gdns   Queen's gdns   London Mews   Devonshire ter
Peel st   Kensington pl   Edge st   Kensington mall   Palace gdns ter   Bayswater Station   Salary   Queensway Station   Craven ter   Leinster ter   Craven hill gdns   Leinster   Craven hill   Lancaster   Craven ter
Campden st   Bedford gdns   Church close   Bark pl   Craven ter   Leinster ter   Craven hill   Lancaster ga
Sheffield ter   Campden hill rd   Tor gdns   Gloucester   **Church street**   Vicarage gdns   Brunswick gdns   Palace Gardens   Palace gdns   Kensington pal gdns   Kensington Palace   **Kensington Gardens**   Lancaster ter   Lancaster ga
Hornton st   Pitt st   Campden   **Church close**   Church   PO   Kensington pal gdns   **Broad Walk**   The Round Pond   Peter Pan Statue   **The Long Water**
ensington   Holland st   Gregory pl   St Mary Abbotts Church   Royal Garden Hotel   Bend Stand   **The Long Water**
ton high street   Kensington Mkt   Barkers   Derry st   **Kensington Station**   Victoria Gate   Palace Gate   WC   **The Temple**
ha   Wright's la   High St Kensington Station   **Kensington road**   Cambridge pl   De Vere gdns   Palace Gate   Bayswater road   Flower Walk   Serpentine Gallery   Restaurant and Snack bar
St Alban's gro   Launceston pl   Victoria   Canning   **Kensington road**   Hyde pk ga   The Flower Walk   Albert Memorial
Kelso   Stanford rd   Cottesmore gdns   Kensington   **Kensington gore**   Prince's gate   Prince's   gdns
Eldon rd   Queen's ga ter   Elvaston pl   Prince Consort rd   Royal College of Organists   Prince's gate
Cornwall   Queen's ga gdns   Royal College of Music   Ennismore gdns   **Knightsbridge**   Knig
well road   Grenville pl   Queen's gate   Imperial College of Science & Technology   Ennismore
Gloucester Rd Station   **South Kensington**   Imperial Institute rd   **Exhibition road**   Prince's   Montpelier   Montp
Courtfield rd   Stanhope gdns   Victoria and Albert Museum   Science Museum   Holy Trinity Church   Montpelier   Cheval pl
Ashburn   Wetherby pl   Clareville st   **Cromwell road**   Victoria & Albert Museum   Thurloe pl   Egerton gdns   Brompton road
Old Brompton-road   **Queen's gate**   Harrington rd   **South Kensington Station**   Alexander   Egerton cres   St Columbas Church
Onslow   Onslow   Cranley pl   Onslow   Melton st   South ter   Pelham st   Egerton ter   Walton st   **Brompton**

© Robert Nicholson Publications
Crown Copyright Reserved

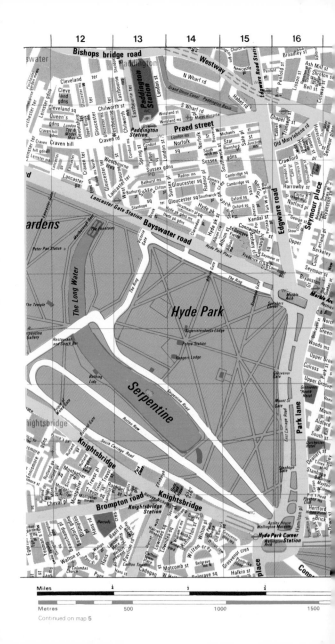

Continued on map 5

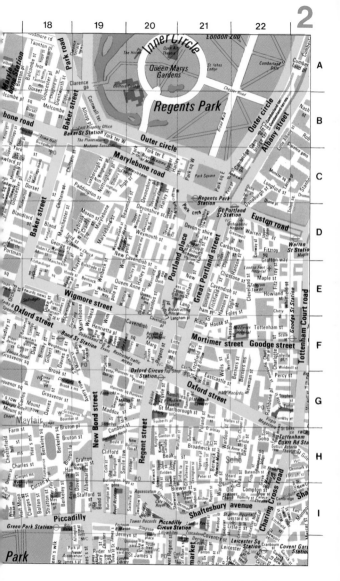

18 **19** **20** **21** **22**

Inner Circle

London Zoo

Queen Marys Gardens

Regents Park

Outer circle

Marylebone road

bone road

Baker St Station

York ter W

York ter E

Outer circle

Albany street

Nash st

Rob

Marylebone road

Park Square

Longford st

Regents Park Station

Gt Portland St Station

Euston road

Euston road

Warren St Station

Baker street

Dorset

Chiltern st

Blandford

Paddington st

Devonshire st

Devonshire st

Weymouth st

New Cavendish st

Portland place

Great Portland street

Carburton

Clipstone st

Fitzroy

Grafton way

Maple

George st

Oxford street

Manchester

Marylebone

Wigmore street

Queen Anne st

New Cavendish st

Cavendish st

Mortimer street

Goodge street

Howland st

Tottenham Court road

Gooden St Station

Portman

sq

Oxford street

Bond St Station

Henrietta pl

Cavendish sq

Langham pl

Mortimer street

Goodge street

Mayfair

Brook st

Grosvenor sq

New Bond street

Hanover

Maddox st

Regent street

Oxford street

Soho

Tottenham Court Rd Station

Conduit st

Broadwick st

Soho

Charing Cross road

Bruton st

Berkeley sq

Clifford st

Shaftesbury avenue

Charles st

Curzon st

Grafton st

Brewer st

Old Compton st

Piccadilly

Green Park Station

Jermyn st

Piccadilly Circus Station

Coventry st

Leicester Sq Station

Leicester

Covent Gar Station

Park

A
B
C
D
E
F
G
H
I

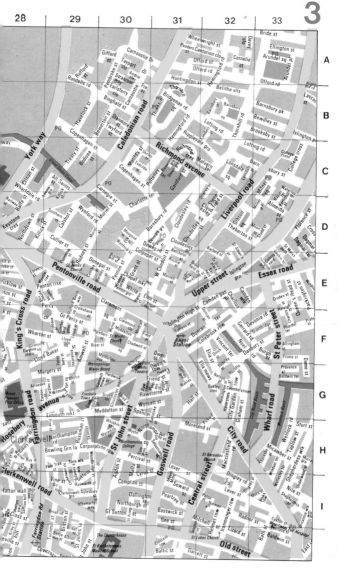

28	29	30	31	32	33

Bride st

A — Wheelwright st · Ponders · Centurion clo · Gifford st · Carnoustie Dr · Taypert · Audrie · Ellington st · Ellington st · PO · Arundel sq pl · Arundel st · Cornelie ct · Offord st · Offord st · Hemingford rd · Rufard · Randells rd · Pembroke · Strassburn · Earlsferry · Bingfield st · Carnoustie clo · Huntingdon st · Belitha vils

B — Havelock st · Bemerton st · Stanmore · Twyford · Copenhagen st · Thornhill · Bridgeman rd · Thornhill · Hemingford rd · Ripplevale gro · Lofting rd · Thornhill rd · Barnsbury · Barnsbury pk · Bewdley st · Brooksby st · Islington pk · York way · Treaty st · Boduca

C — All Saints · PO · Caledonian road · Copenhagen st · Richmond avenue · Matilda · Everilda · Putney · Maygood · Malvern · Gaunton st · Lonsdale sq · Barn · sbury sq · College cross · College cross · Wharfdale rd · Carnegie st · Charlotte st

D — Railway · Northdown st · Calshot st · Collier st · Wynford rd · Muriel st · Barnsbury rd · Cloudesley sq · Cloudesley · Liverpool road · Theberton st · Gibson · Almeida · Milner · Waterloo · Florence st · Cross · Keystone cres · Killick st · Maygood · Wynford rd · Dewey rd · Barnsbury · Cloudesley · Barnsbury · Dagmar · Dagmar te · St Marys

E — ld hall · ntville st · ton st · icklow st · Pentonville road · Penton rise · Penton st · St James · Church · Chapel mkt · W Cubitt st · Donegal st · White · Lyon st · Upper street · Islington grn · Camden pas · Charlton · Essex road · Islington grn · Camden pas · Mantell

F — King's Cross road · Percy · cir · Gt Percy st · Wharton st · Cruikshank · Myddelton · Claremont · sq · Pleasant · Lloyd · River st · Chadwell st · Islington High · Torrens st · Duncan · ter · Colebrook row · Gerrard rd · Vincent ter · Noel · Devonia rd · Grambridge · Burgh · St Peter street · Allingham · Frome st · Wharton st · Ingleber st · St Marks · Church · Angel · Statue · Danbury st · Nuen st · Rheidol · Granville sq · Gwynne pl · Amwell st

G — Lloyd Baker · Margery st · Martin · Ampton · Myddelton · Water Board · Sadlers · Wells · Theatre · Owen · Owen st · Friend st · Rawstone st · Wynatt st · Spencer st · Hall st · City Garden · Graham st · Wharf road · Provence st · Baldwin ter · Atneave · Wilmington · Finsbury · Tower Hall · Greenhurst · Moon st · Ella mews · Oakley · cres · Nelson · Rodnie · Coombs street · Mount · Pleasant · Post Office · Exmouth mkt · Myddelton sq

H — Rosebery · Clerkenwell · Farringdon road · avenue · sant · Clerkenwell road · Northampton rd · Bowling Grn la · Corporation row · St John street · Northampton Sq · Northampton row · Moreland st · St Barnabas Church · City road · Macclesfield · Dingley rd · Wenlock · Micawber st · Sturt st · Taplow st · Shepherdess wlk · Whiskin · Meredith · Rosoman st · Wynyatt · Pear Tree · Ray st · Sans wlk · Percival st · Lever st

I — Clerkenwell road · atton wall · Cross · n · ville st · Farringdon Rd · Station · Vine st · br · Clerkenwell Aylesbury · grn · Broad yd · St John's · Bit · Benja Alb · st · Compton st · Dallington st · Northburgh st · Gt Sutton st · Cowcross · Hayward's · Albemarle · The Charterhouse · St Bartholomews · Medical School · Seward st · Peartree st · Bastwick st · Gee st · PO · Lever st · Central street · Ironmonger row · Radnor st · Mitchell · Lizard st · St Lukes Church · Old street · Baltic st · Garnett st · Crescent · Bath · Baldwin st · Nile st · Sheperdess · wlk · Hospital · East

© Robert Nicholson Publications
Crown Copyright Reserved

Continued on map 1

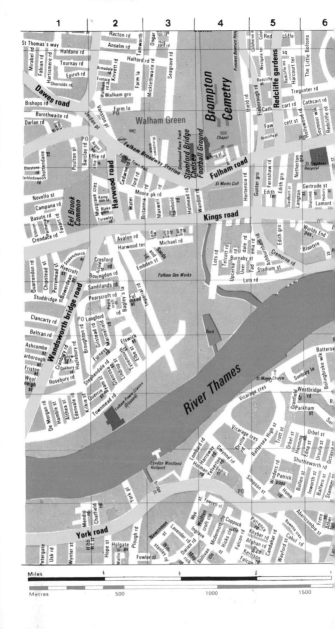

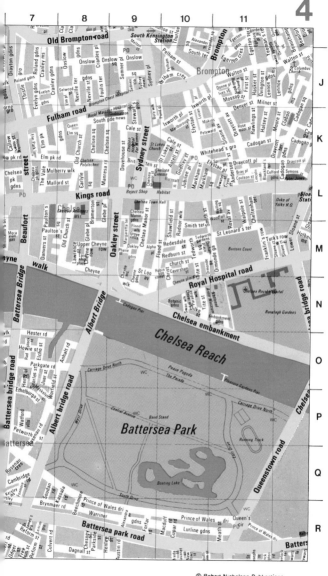

4

7 **8** **9** **10** **11**

Old Brompton road
South Kensington Station

J

Fulham road

K

Kings road

Sydney street

L

Beaufort street
Oakley street

M

Cheyne walk

Royal Hospital road

N

Battersea Bridge
Albert Bridge
Chelsea embankment

O

Chelsea Reach

Battersea bridge road
Albert bridge road

P

Battersea Park

Queenstown road

Q

R

Prince of Wales dri
Battersea park road

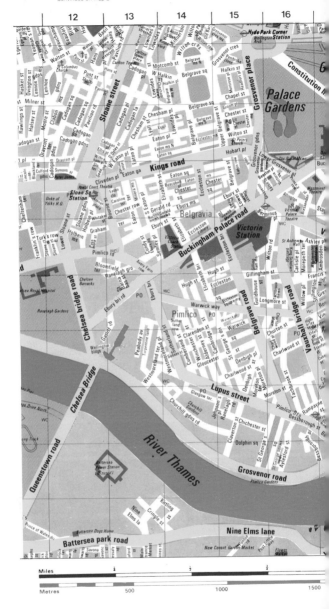

12   13   14   15   16

Hyde Park Corner
Wellington Station
Wellington Arch

Constitution h

Palace Gardens

Grosvenor place

Sloane street

Kings road

Royal Court Theatre
Sloan Sq Station

Duke of Yorks H.Q.

Belgravia

Buckingham Palace road

Victoria Station

Belgrave road

Vauxhall bridge road

Chelsea bridge road

Chelsea Royal Hospital

Ranelagh Gardens

Pimlico

Warwick way

Chelsea Bridge

Lupus street

Wellington bldgs

Queenstown road

River Thames

Battersea Power Station (disused)

Grosvenor road
Pimlico Gardens

Nine Elms la

Cringle st

Kirtling

Nine Elms lane

Battersea park road

Battersea Dogs Home

New Covent Garden Market

Prince of Wales dr

Miles   ¼   ½   ¾

Metres   500   1000   1500

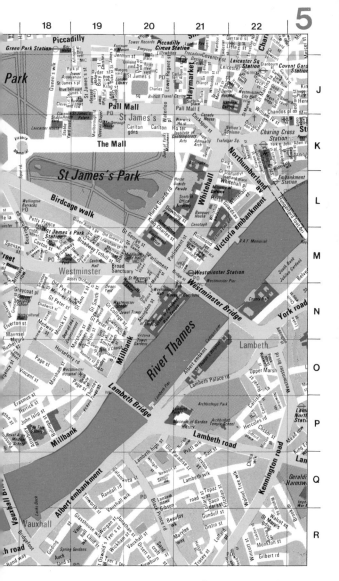

Piccadilly

Green Park Station

Tower Records   Piccadilly   London
Fortnum   Simpson   Circus Station
Lillywhites
Jermyn st   Coventry st   Leicester Sq
Trocadero   Leicester   Station   Covent Garden
Design   sq   Station
Centre
Haymarket   PD   Whitcomb st   Westminster
Charles   City Hall   Chandos pl
British Travel Centre   Charing Cross

Park

Queen's wlk   Arlington st   Bennett st
Park pl
Travel   MCC
Association   Ryder st   Bury st   Masons yd   Apple tree yd
St James's pl   Duke of York st
King st   Jermyn st
Blue Ball yd
Clev   Russell   St James's sq
St James's   Square
Clarence   St James's   Pall Mall   PO   Waterloo pl   Pall Mall E
House   Stable   Palace
Lancaster House   Stable Yd Rd   Marlborough   Marlborough   Warwick   Canada
rd   House   Carlton   Carlton   ho ter   House
gdns   Cockspur st   Nelson's
Column
Duke of York's   Trafalgar Sq.
Institute of
Contemporary   Admiralty   Charing Cross
Arts   Arch   Station

Pall Mall

St James's

Victoria
Memorial

The Mall

St James's Park

Northumberland

Embankment
Station

Birdcage walk

Horse Guards
Parade   Gt Scotland place
Scottish   Whitehall   Whitehall pl
Office   Horse
Banqueting   Guards av
House   Richmond   R.A.F. Memorial
ter
Victoria embankment
Cenotaph

Wellington
Barracks   PO
Petty France   St   St James's Park   Queen Anne's ga   Gt George st
Station   Lewisham st   King Charles st
Carton st   Broadway   Tothill   Downing st
Broadway   st   Parliament st   Parliament   Scotland
Spenser   Caxton st
st   St   Storey's ga   sq

Westminster   Central   Broad
Hall   Sanctuary   Bridge   Westminster Station
Abbey   Yard   Westminster Pier
Greycoat pl   Old Pye st   St   Westminster

Greycoat   St Ann's st   Gt Smith   Gt College st   Victoria
School   Chadwick st   Gt Peter st   Tower   South Bank
Jewel Tower   Gardens   Jubilee Gardens
Medway   Gt Peter st   Abingdon st
Elverton st   Marsham   Tufton   Smith   Millbank
st   st   sq   Westminster   Belve
Maunsel   Horseferry rd   Hospital   County Hall
st   Page st
Rutherford   Page st
Vincent st   Marshall
Page st   Victoria Tower   Millbank
st   Gardens   Lambeth

River Thames   York road

Lambeth

Erasmus st
John Islip st   Upper Marsh
Herrick st

Albert embankment   Lambeth Pier

Millbank   Royal Army   Lambeth Palace rd
Medical School   Lambeth Bridge
Lambeth   Lam
North
Archbishops Park   Station

Museum of Garden   Archbishops
History   Temple School
Cossor st
Lambeth road   Hercules rd   Mead row

Randall rd   Lambeth high st   Old Paradise st   Pratt wlk   Sail st   China   King
wlk   Lan
Lambeth wlk   Ken
Salamanca st   Lambeth   Geraldine
Vauxhall wlk   Black   Prince rd   road   Saun   Harmsw
PO   Gibson   ders   Imper
Vauxhall   st   War M

Vauxhall

Albert embankment

Glasshouse   Worgan st   Tyer's st   Vauxhall   Beaufoy   Gundulf st   Walcot sq
Auck   st   Wickham st   Distin   st   St Mary's
Bridgefoot   Vaux hall   wlk   Vauxhall st   Oswald   Tyer's st   Marlee   way   Monkton st   gdns
h road   Godding   Spring Gardens   Newburn   st   Tracey   st   Lollard   st   Gilbert rd
Bond way   land st   Dorset   st   Sans   Beaufoy

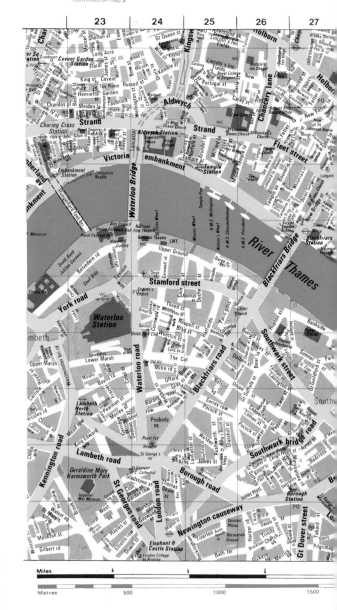

| 23 | 24 | 25 | 26 | 27 |

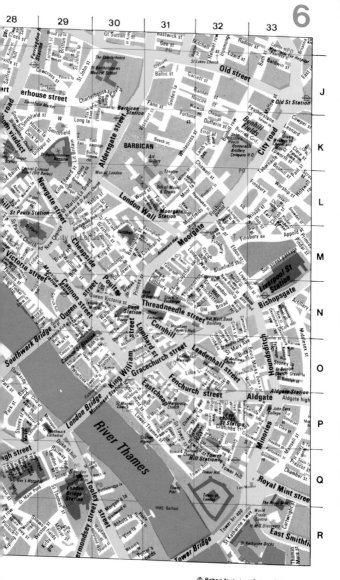

Theatres

Adelphi 836 7611
Albery 836 3878
Aldwych 836 6404
Ambassadors 836 6111
Apollo 437 2663
Apollo Victoria 828 8665
Astoria 437 8772
Bloomsbury 387 9629
Coliseum 836 3161
Comedy 930 2578
Criterion 930 3216
Donmar Warehouse 240 8230
Dominion 580 9562
Drury Lane 836 8108
Duchess 836 8243
Duke of York's 836 5122
Fortune 836 2238
Garrick 836 4601
Globe 437 1592
Haymarket 930 9832
Her Majesty's 930 6606
ICA 930 0493
Jeannetta Cochrane 242 7040
Lyric 437 3686
Mayfair 629 3036
Mermaid 236 5568
National Theatre 928 2252
New London 405 0072
Old Vic 928 7616
Palace 434 0909
Palladium 437 7373
Phoenix 836 2294
Piccadilly 437 4506
Prince Edward 734 8951
Prince of Wales 839 5987
Queen's 734 1166
Royal Court 730 1745
Royal Festival Hall 928 3191
Royal Opera House 240 1066
Sadler's Wells 278 8916
St Martin's 836 1443
Savoy 836 8888
Shaftesbury 379 5399
Strand 836 2660
Vaudeville 836 9988
Victoria Palace 834 1317
Westminster 834 0283
Whitehall 930 7765
Wigmore Hall 935 2141
Wyndham 836 3028
Young Vic 928 6363

Cinemas

Cannon (Haymarket) 839 1527
Cannon (Oxford St) 636 0310
Cannon (Panton St) 930 0631
Cannon (Piccadilly) 437 3561
Cannon Premiere 439 4770
Cannon Royal 930 6915
Cannon (Shaftesbury Av) 836 8861
Cannon (Tott Ct Rd) 636 6148
Curzon (Mayfair) 499 3737
Curzon (Phoenix) 240 9661
Curzon (West End) 439 4805
Dominion 580 9562
Empire 1,2 & 3 437 1234
ICA 930 3647
Leicester Sq Theatre 930 5252
Lumiere 836 0691
Metro 437 0757
Minema 235 4225
Moulin 437 1653
National Film Theatre 928 3232
Odeon (Haymarket) 839 7697
Odeon (Leicester Sq) 930 6111
Odeon (Marble Arch) 723 2011
Plaza 1,2,3 & 4 200 0200
Prince Charles 439 3657
Renoir 837 8402
Roxie 437 8181
Warner West End 439 0791

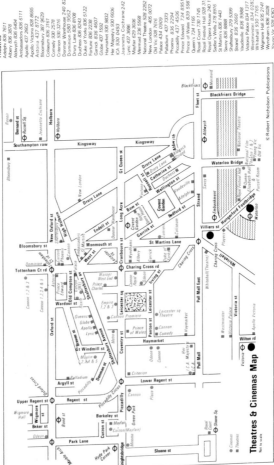

Theatres & Cinemas Map

Not to scale

© Robert Nicholson Publications

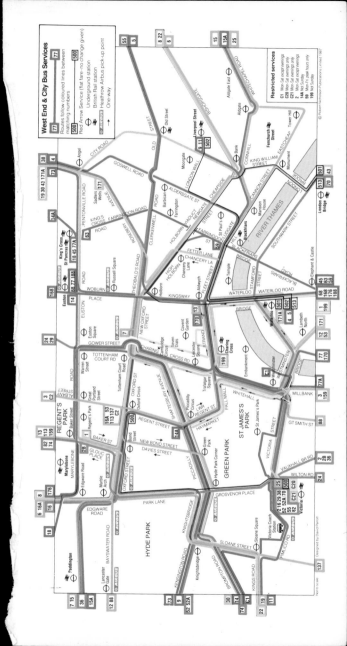

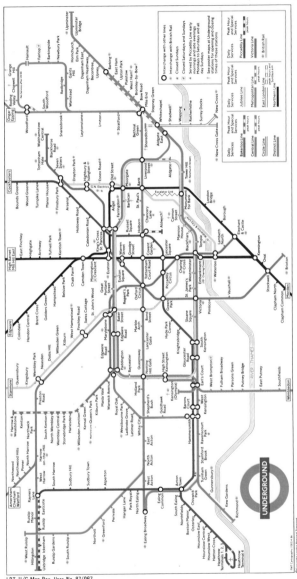

LRT U/G Map Reg. User No. 87/067